Quality and Choice:
A decent home for all

The way forward for housing

December 2000

...nment, Transport and the Regions
...curity

Department of the Environment, Transport and the Regions
Eland House
Bressenden Place
London SW1E 5DU
Telephone 020 7944 3000
Internet service http://www.detr.gov.uk/

Further copies of this report are available from:

Department of the Environment, Transport and the Regions
Publications Sale Centre
Unit 21
Goldthorpe Industrial Estate
Goldthorpe
Rotherham S63 9BL
Tel: 01709 891318
Fax: 01709 881673

ISBN 851124 63 2

You may also access this document at the Department's web site: www.housing.detr.gov.uk

Printed in the UK on material containing 75% post-consumer waste and 25% ECF pulp (cover) and
100% post-consumer waste (text).

December 2000

CONTENTS

Foreword

by the Deputy Prime Minister

In April this year I launched our Housing Green Paper. Entitled *Quality and Choice: a Decent Home for All*, it was the first comprehensive review of housing for 23 years. It set out a strategy to achieve our aim that everyone should have the opportunity of a decent home. And it communicated our policies for giving people much greater involvement in, and control over, their housing choices.

This document explains how we are taking the agenda forward in the light of the consultation. As with the Green Paper it covers the whole range of housing issues including Housing Benefit, for which Alistair Darling is responsible.

I wrote in April that I looked forward to the debate that our Green Paper would stimulate. I have not been disappointed. The debate has been lively and constructive, but overwhelmingly supportive of our approach. The verdict is that we got it about right.

Now there is much to do. Indeed we have already started. In July we announced a significant increase in resources for housing. This, added to previous increases, will set us on course to ensuring that all social homes will meet set standards of decency within a decade.

This document sets out how we are pursuing a number of ideas in the Green Paper. Our Starter Home Initiative will help key workers realise their aspirations of home ownership where they have been priced out of the market. We are legislating to modernise the home buying and selling process to tackle gazumping and other problems. We are providing stronger statutory protection for the homeless. We want to give more effective support to some home owners who do not have the means to repair their homes. We are piloting lettings schemes that give social tenants greater involvement in their choice of home. We are reforming social rents so that what people pay bears more relationship to what they get; but we are keeping rents affordable. We are making the Housing Benefit system work harder for those that need it. And we continue to press for all private landlords to match the standards of the best.

I hope you will be inspired by our policies and excited by our agenda. Above all I hope you will play your part in taking the agenda forward. I commend this document to you.

John Prescott
Deputy Prime Minister

Summary

1. This document sets out our policies to achieve the Government's aim to offer everyone the opportunity of a decent home and so promote social cohesion, well-being and self-dependence. It follows up the Housing Green Paper, 'Quality and Choice: A Decent Home for All', published in April 2000.

2. The Green Paper invited views on our strategy for housing in England. Subsequently, in July, we announced a substantial increase in housing investment which will enable us to deliver our strategy. By 2003/04 annual capital investment in housing will be £4 billion, compared with just over £1.5 billion planned spending in 1997/98.

3. The main themes of the Green Paper were quality and choice. Quality through better homes and better services. Choice through people being given greater involvement in, and control over, their housing. Across all types of housing, owned or rented, private or public, our policies are intended to deliver improvements in quality and a fairer system which together allow people to make real choices about their homes, which support people moving into work and self-dependence, and which protect the vulnerable.

4. The Green Paper and this statement are integral parts of our wider agenda to revitalise urban and rural areas and tackle social exclusion. They need to be read alongside a number of other policy statements that have been published this year, notably: the Urban and Rural White Papers; the National Strategy for Neighbourhood Renewal; and the Planning Policy Guidance note for housing (PPG3).

5. The key proposals in the Green Paper were:

    -   a stronger, more strategic role for local authorities, across all housing in their area, public and private;

    -   additional measures to support sustainable home ownership, including a Starter Home Initiative for key workers, extra support for home owners moving from welfare to work and more flexible forms of assistance for private housing renovation;

    -   measures to raise the standards of private rented housing, encourage new investment and tackle problems at the bottom end of the sector;

    -   a range of investment and management measures to bring all social housing up to a decent standard by 2010 and tackle fuel poverty among social housing tenants;

    -   measures to deliver new affordable housing in line with local needs;

    -   reforms to lettings policies for social housing to promote a more customer-focused approach;

    -   increased protection of unintentionally homeless people in priority need;

    -   a review of tenure arrangements for social housing, retaining security for long term social tenants;

- reforms to establish a fairer system of rents for tenants of local authorities and registered social landlords;

- measures to streamline and simplify the administration of Housing Benefit, tackle fraud and improve work incentives; and

- steps to tackle other forms of social exclusion, including rough sleeping, fuel poverty and anti-social behaviour.

6.   We set out here our housing policies in the light of the Green Paper and the consultation responses. And we describe how we intend to implement our policies.

7.   The Green Paper was welcomed by an overwhelming majority of the 1,099 respondents. There has been a lively debate on some of the proposals and much valuable comment and constructive criticism. We have sought to take account of this in formulating our policies. Some proposals have been modified to reflect concerns expressed during the consultation period. The following chapters of this document set out in more detail the way in which we are moving forward. Our key measures are summarised below:

Making it work locally

8.   The Green Paper stressed how important it is that local delivery of housing policies is tailored to local circumstances. These vary widely between different areas, reflecting the diversity of our communities and the level of demand for housing. We placed a particular emphasis on the need for local authorities to take a stronger strategic role in housing, meeting needs across all types of housing and integrating housing policy with wider social, economic and environmental policies. This policy statement sets the national framework within which local authorities should work.

9.   Four specific measures which we are taking forward to enhance the strategic role are:

- increasing local authorities' resources and giving them greater flexibility to adopt policies that meet the needs of their communities across all types of housing;

- providing guidance to enable local authorities to carry out proper needs assessments and stock condition surveys to underpin their housing strategies;

- developing closer partnership working between the Housing Corporation and local authorities, in particular ensuring that investment in new social housing meets local priorities; and

- encouraging collaboration between neighbouring local authorities to ensure that problems are tackled effectively and not shifted from place to place, including the problems of low demand housing.

10.   A number of our proposals for greater quality and choice in private and social housing will contribute to these improvements.

Encouraging sustainable home ownership

11. We support sustainable home ownership. This means a framework where owners can afford the commitments of ownership in the long term. The biggest contribution we can make is to create a strong and stable economy, avoiding the boom and bust of the past. In the Housing Green Paper we described existing proposals to improve the home buying and selling process, to introduce a new tenure, commonhold, and reform of leasehold and proposed a new home ownership scheme, the Starter Home Initiative. We also proposed reforms to the ways in which we support home owners who lose their jobs and how we provide assistance for the renovation of private sector housing.

12. We have developed these proposals since the Green Paper was published and will:

    * press ahead with a range of initiatives to improve the home buying and selling process, including legislation in 2000/01 to require sellers to prepare a seller's information pack before their homes are marketed;

    * legislate to introduce commonhold and reform leasehold;

    * introduce the Starter Home Initiative in 2001, to help around 10,000 key workers, particularly teachers, nurses and the police, to buy their own homes in high price, high demand areas. We are today inviting organisations to bid for a share of the £250 million subsidy available over the next three years;

    * help unemployed home owners to move into work through improvements to benefit support for mortgages, paying extra support for a limited period after a person takes up employment. This extra support will be available from April 2001; and

    * give greater discretion to local authorities to enable them to support the renovation and improvement of private sector housing in a better targeted, more strategic way. Authorities will be given greater flexibility to use grants and loans to support home repair, and more effective powers to turn round areas of low demand and unpopular housing.

Promoting a healthy private rented sector

13. Our Housing Green Paper contained a number of proposals to raise the standards of reputable private landlords, encourage new investment and tackle problems at the bottom end of the sector.

14. The key measures we are taking forward to improve standards are:

    * helping well-intentioned landlords to improve their expertise through voluntary accreditation schemes and other best practice initiatives;

    * legislating as soon as Parliamentary time allows to introduce a compulsory licensing system for Houses in Multiple Occupation and consulting on proposals for selective licensing of private landlords in areas of low demand. We will also work up, for consultation, options for Housing Benefit measures which could be linked to our licensing proposals.

- continuing to consider whether there are any tax measures which could make long-term investment in private rented housing a more attractive proposition; and

- introducing a new health and safety rating scale for assessing the condition of homes in all tenures.

Raising the quality of social housing

15. The Housing Green Paper set out our strategy to improve the quality of social housing and our commitment to bring all social housing up to a decent standard within ten years. In July we announced extra resources both for local authorities to invest in their stock where they choose to retain it and for other options.

16. In taking these proposals forward, we will:

- bring all social housing up to a decent standard by 2010. We have set a Public Service Agreement target to improve a third of the homes that don't meet that standard by March 2004;

- ensure that local authorities adopt a more business-like approach to housing management and investment through a new financial framework with a new Major Repairs Allowance of £1.6 billion from 2001/02 to cover the cost of maintaining council housing in sound condition, and through the application of the recommendations of the Construction Task Force in 'Rethinking Construction';

- support the transfer of up to 200,000 homes each year from local authorities to registered social landlords, where proposals are supported by tenants;

- encourage the creation of new arms-length management arrangements for local authority housing. In 2002/03 and 2003/04 authorities which have established such arrangements will be given extra scope to borrow for investment where there is a proven record of excellence in management and a clear business plan for the stock. Up to £460 million is being made available for this scheme;

- promote new Private Finance Initiative schemes for local authority housing worth an extra £600 million in 2002/03 and 2003/04; and

- ensure the consistent and rigorous application of Best Value and Tenant Participation Compact principles across all social housing.

Providing new affordable housing

17. The Housing Green Paper set out our aim to deliver new affordable housing where it is needed and in a form that is sustainable. Our proposals for achieving this included a strategic use of the Housing Corporation's Approved Development Programme (ADP) as well as effective use of planning powers. In taking our proposals forward we will:

- increase investment in affordable housing through the ADP to over £1.2 billion by 2003/04, almost double current levels. This funding is in addition to money for affordable housing provided by local authorities and through the Starter Home Initiative;

- distribute funds from the Housing Corporation's ADP more in line with the priorities in regional housing statements and local housing strategies, so that investment matches local needs;

- apply the Construction Task Force's recommendations and other new construction techniques to Housing Corporation-funded developments to ensure greater efficiency, better design and higher quality; and

- produce best practice guidance for local authorities to encourage more effective use of planning powers for the provision of affordable housing within new private developments.

Promoting choice through lettings in social housing

18. In the Housing Green Paper we said that social landlords should provide a more customer focused service. We proposed reforms to lettings policies which would offer choice, tackle social exclusion, help create sustainable communities and encourage the effective use and management of social housing.

19. We will do this by:

- legislating in 2000/01 to facilitate choice-based lettings policies;

- providing £11 million over the next three years to fund pilot lettings schemes that are customer-focused and choice-based; and

- promoting choice based lettings schemes more generally.

Strengthening the protection available to the homeless

20. The Housing Green Paper set out our proposals to improve the protection for priority need groups who become homeless through no fault of their own. We intend to proceed with these proposals.

21. Our key measures are:

- legislating in 2000/01, placing a stronger duty on local housing authorities to accommodate people who are homeless through no fault of their own and who are in priority need;

- extending by order the groups of vulnerable homeless people who have a priority need for accommodation (such as care leavers and others with an institutionalised background, the victims of domestic violence and 16 & 17 year-olds);

- legislating in 2000/01, to give housing authorities the power to provide accommodation for people who are homeless through no fault of their own but do not have priority need, where sufficient housing is available; and

- legislating in 2000/01, to require housing authorities to conduct a homelessness review, prepare a homelessness strategy, and take measures to prevent homelessness, as part of their housing strategy.

22. Together with our legislative measures to improve lettings schemes, these measures will provide a comprehensive, properly integrated framework for offering settled housing to homeless people and others in housing need.

New forms of tenure for social housing

23. The Housing Green Paper confirmed our belief that the security of tenure enjoyed by social housing tenants should not be reduced. We proposed to look at the benefits of, and options for, a new single form of tenure for the social rented sector and also at creating new flexibilities for landlords to make better use of their stock. Of those who commented on our proposals for a review the majority supported the case for a single form of tenure. We will consider these proposals further but do not propose any significant change to the Right To Buy.

Moving to a fairer system of affordable social rents

24. The Housing Green Paper set out our aim of bringing greater fairness and coherence to the structure of social rents. We also gave a commitment to keep social rents at affordable levels, well below rent levels in the private sector. A more coherent pattern of rents would support our wider aims to give tenants more choice and more of a say over the homes in which they live.

25. There was broad agreement that the current structure of rents is incoherent and desperately in need of reform. But it has proved less easy to secure consensus on the means to the end.

26. We have developed an approach which bases a property's rent on its size, its value compared to other social properties and the earnings in the surrounding area. In future, people who live in properties which are smaller, in poorer condition, or in less attractive locations should have lower rents than those in more advantageous circumstances. There should not be arbitrary differences in rents between similar properties in similar areas.

27. The new approach will be put in place over a ten-year period. Some tenants will see their rents go down. There will be rises for others, but any rises will not exceed £2 a week in any year above normal inflation-linked increases. Landlords will have some flexibility over how changes are implemented and we will expect them to consult their tenants. Housing Benefit will continue to meet in full the eligible rents of tenants on income support or Job Seeker's Allowance.

28. These reforms will help to create a social sector where rents are fair. We are looking to landlords to ensure that, in partnership with their tenants, our policy to develop a fairer and more reasonable pattern of rents is successfully delivered in detail at the local level.

29. We also want to achieve the right balance between the average rents charged by local authorities and registered social landlords. Achieving this balance will require local

authority rents to rise slightly faster than the rate of inflation over the next ten years or so but still at a slower rate than in recent years. This will coincide with the continued improvement of the condition of local authority stock to ensure that all unsatisfactory council housing is brought up to a decent standard within ten years.

30. In summary, the key elements of our rents policy are:

- keeping social rents below market levels and based on size, relative property values and local earnings;

- ensuring that no tenant's rent increases by more than £2 per week per year above the normal inflation-linked increases;

- that overall rent increases for registered social landlords should be no more than ½% above inflation in any year from 2002/03; and

- achieving a coherent structure for social rents within ten years, but giving social landlords some flexibility over detailed implementation.

Improving Housing Benefit

31. Housing Benefit has an important role both in terms of our welfare to work and social exclusion agenda and our wider housing objectives. We have listened and have concluded that there is a need for action on two main fronts;

- to **raise standards in administration** – by raising standards across the board, but also helping struggling authorities improve; and

- to **simplify the system** – by reforming the Single Room Rent and exploring scope for simplifying both the claims process and the 4 parallel schemes that are currently in place.

32. Action on both these fronts will promote better administration and better work incentives.

33. Our key measures are:

- raising standards in Housing Benefit administration and promoting work incentives, working with local authorities;

- setting up our expert team to help struggling local authorities tackle immediate problems, along with action to improve the situation of registered social landlords;

- developing and implementing a new performance management framework to raise standards across the board and link local authority performance to funding;

- promoting work incentives for young people through reform of the Single Room Rent;

- making Housing Benefit both easier to administer and easier to claim by streamlining and simplifying the process for making claims, and ensuring the rules are compatible with Tax Credits;

- simplifying Housing Benefit by further exploring simplification of the 4 transitional protection schemes.

34. In addition, we are giving further consideration to options for reforming housing support over the long-term. For example, we will look in more detail at the issues raised by respondents commenting on a scheme with a flat-rate element, as well as listen to ideas raised during our consultation on the Pension Credit.

Tackling other forms of housing-related social exclusion

35. The Housing Green Paper emphasised the important part that decent homes can play in promoting social cohesion. Chapter 12 of the Green Paper set out our policies for tackling a range of housing-related forms of social exclusion.

36. In taking our proposals and policies forward, we will continue to support vulnerable members of society and others who may be socially excluded. We want to ensure that everyone has the opportunity of a decent home and the support they need to achieve the quality of life that most enjoy.

37. The key policies set out in this statement to tackle other forms of social exclusion are:

- our ambitious programme to reduce the numbers of people sleeping rough by two-thirds between 1998 & 2002, implementing the strategy of the Rough Sleepers Unit, 'Coming in from the Cold';

- our new Supporting People programme, to improve the quality, range and flexibility of support services to vulnerable people, with £138 million of implementation funding and £137 million for new services under our Safer Communities Supported Housing Fund;

- our strategy to tackle fuel poverty through the new Home Energy Efficiency Scheme and other programmes;

- our new programme to improve the quality of Gypsy sites; and

- our national drive to tackle anti-social behaviour, taking forward the recommendations of Policy Action Team 8 which was set up as part of the Social Exclusion Unit's work on neighbourhood renewal.

Implementation

38. This statement sets out a comprehensive package of policies for housing in England. Together with the additional resources we are making available they will lead to a major improvement in the quality of life for many people in this country. We will keep track of how well we are delivering improvements by setting targets, as appropriate, against which performance can be assessed, and developing an evaluation programme for our policies. We look to those in the private, public and voluntary sectors to join us over the next decade and beyond in implementing these policies and ensuring that everyone has the opportunity – and choice – of a decent home.

Introduction

1. On 4 April we published our Housing Green Paper *Quality and Choice: A Decent Home for All*. The Green Paper contained a strategy to ensure that everyone has the opportunity of a decent home. It set out a number of new proposals which, along with previously announced policies, covered the whole range of housing choices from social housing through to owner occupation.

2. The Green Paper has stimulated a lively and constructive debate. Over 1,000 organisations and individuals submitted responses, many of them comprehensive. A number of bodies, ranging from national organisations to individual local authorities, organised conferences and seminars to discuss the Green Paper and there have been numerous articles in the housing and national press focusing on specific proposals.

3. The Department commissioned independent consultants to analyse the responses to the Green Paper. Their analysis is being made available on the Department's website. The consultants note that: "Out of 1,099 responses only seven respondents disagree fundamentally with the principles and aims of the Green Paper. The proposals on the whole are seen as a considered effort to raise the standards of housing throughout the country and throughout different tenures".

4. This policy statement sets out our strategy to deliver improvements to the quality of housing and to enhance people's housing choices. It concentrates on proposals introduced or developed in the Green Paper and takes stock of progress on existing proposals. It should be read in conjunction with the Green Paper, which sets out more fully the principles that underpin our policies.

5. This statement should also be read in the context of the Government's wider objectives. This year has seen us reach a number of milestones in developing our social and economic agenda. Earlier in the year we published, for consultation, the National Strategy for Neighbourhood Renewal. An Action Plan reflecting the consultation will be published in the near future; this will set out how we are tackling the problems of deprived areas. And we have just published two White Papers, *Our Towns and Cities – the Future* and *Our Countryside – The Future* setting out the Government's vision and policies for Urban and Rural areas. Our goal is to improve the quality of life for everybody, wherever they live, by creating more sustainable communities that put people first. And decent homes are a basic requirement for any community.

6. We will implement the changes in policy set out in this statement as quickly as possible.

7. Some of our proposals require investment. Our spending plans, announced in July, provide the additional resources necessary to take these proposals forward over the next three years. In our 2000 Spending Review we looked closely at our priorities for housing in the context of the Green Paper and the many initial comments we received in response to it. We concluded that, despite the higher levels of investment planned in 2001/02, more resources would be needed to fulfil the commitments in the Green Paper. We are providing substantial increases. By 2003/04 capital investment in housing will have risen to more than £4 billion, compared with planned spending of £1.5 billion in 1997/98.

8.   Some proposals require legislation. We have announced our intention to legislate on home buying and selling and homelessness during the current (2000/01) Parliamentary session. We will implement the other legislative proposals as soon as Parliamentary time allows.

9.   To implement many of our proposals we shall be producing guidance and encouraging change through partnerships between local authorities, landlords, lenders, house builders, home owners, tenants and others involved in housing. We will keep track of how well we are delivering improvements by setting targets, as appropriate, against which performance can be assessed, and developing an evaluation programme for our policies and initiatives.

10.   This statement sets the framework for housing policy in England for the next decade and beyond. Parts of it still need to be worked up in detail but the general thrust of the policy is clear. Across all types of housing, owned or rented, private or public, our policies are intended to deliver improvements in quality and choice, supporting people moving into work and self-reliance, and protecting the vulnerable.

Housing policy and the devolved administrations

11.   This is a housing policy statement for England, although a number of changes to primary legislation would affect both England and Wales. Changes to Housing Benefit and benefit support for mortgage interest payments would also apply in Northern Ireland, Scotland and Wales and are subject to separate consultation between the Department of Social Security and the devolved administrations.

12.   The National Assembly for Wales will consult shortly on a National Housing Strategy for Wales which will set out its proposals for Welsh housing policy. That strategy will take account of the proposals in the Green Paper as they affect Wales. The National Assembly will be closely involved in the preparation of any primary legislation which will affect Wales. Where detailed implementation is by means of secondary legislation, the Assembly will be able to use their powers to deliver the most appropriate implementation in Wales, in line with their National Housing Strategy.

13.   The Scottish Executive will introduce a Housing Bill to the Scottish Parliament before Christmas. This will provide the foundations for the most radical restructuring of Scotland's housing for a generation, embedding principles of social justice and equality of opportunity for all, and helping to achieve the Executive's overall aim of fostering successful balanced communities, with high quality affordable houses to rent and to purchase. Specifically, the Bill will include measures promoting tenants' rights; facilitating community ownership of housing; tackling homelessness; strengthening the strategic role of local authorities; and delivering high quality housing services across Scotland.

14.   In Northern Ireland, the Minister for Social Development is aiming to introduce a Housing Bill which will build upon and develop existing legislation in a number of areas, particularly private sector renewal, powers of the Housing Executive (the sole public housing authority for Northern Ireland) tenants' rights and anti-social behaviour.

CHAPTER ONE

Making it work locally

Our Key Measures are:

- To increase local authorities' resources and give them greater flexibility to adopt policies that meet the needs of their communities across all types of housing

- To provide guidance to enable local authorities to carry out proper needs assessments and stock condition surveys to underpin their housing strategies

- To develop closer partnership working between the Housing Corporation and local authorities, in particular ensuring that investment in new social housing meets local priorities

- To encourage collaboration between neighbouring local authorities to ensure that problems are tackled effectively and not shifted from place to place, including the problems of low demand housing

---

What the Green Paper said

1.1   In chapter 3 of the Green Paper, we set out our ambition to see local authorities exercising a strategic role covering all local factors affecting housing provision, and separating that strategic role from landlord responsibilities. This was based on our recognition of the importance of housing to people's wider health and well-being, the need to tailor local solutions to local circumstances and the diversity of communities.

What consultees said

1.2   There was overwhelming support for the continuation and development of a strategic role for local authorities. Many respondents highlighted the importance of more comprehensive assessments of local housing need, noting that housing cannot be considered in isolation. A number of respondents raised the need for resources to develop the strategic role, both financial and in terms of skills. Not many respondents commented specifically on the separation of the strategic and landlord roles of local authorities.

Our policy approach

1.3   We have been pleased to see many in the local authority world engaging with the issues. Before the launch of the Green Paper the Local Government Association established a task group to consider how to develop the strategic role of local authorities. We wish to encourage this thinking. In particular we continue to believe there are benefits to be derived from separating the strategic role from the role of housing management. Some local authorities may wish to pursue the option of putting their housing management operations at arm's length, even if they are not availing themselves of the extra borrowing possibilities proposed in Chapter 7 of the Green Paper.

1.4   We recognise that different local authorities face different problems. The objectives and priorities that they set out in their housing strategies will reflect important local differences. But it is important that local authorities take account of national and regional priorities too. Local authorities should develop housing strategies that set out their long term objectives and targets and how these will be achieved. These will need to be linked to other related responsibilities, such as those for regeneration. As part of this process local authorities will have to assess local needs and decide local priorities. They will need to consult their residents and take proper account of the needs of black and ethnic minorities, rural and other such communities.

1.5   It is also important for neighbouring local authorities to collaborate and share their local housing strategies to ensure that any problems identified, such as low demand, are tackled and not merely shifted from one local authority to another. This is particularly important where housing markets cross over local authority boundaries.

1.6   The Local Government Act 2000 introduced a new duty on local authorities to prepare a community strategy to promote or improve the economic, social and environmental well-being of their areas. This new requirement will be important in bringing together local authorities, agencies and private and voluntary sectors into strategic partnerships to plan and deliver the steps necessary to improve all aspects of local quality of life. These local strategic partnerships, which will prepare the community strategies, will provide a single local co-ordination framework to make sure that services, in particular core public services, work together. Housing is a key element in determining quality of life. The housing strategies produced by local authorities should therefore form an important component of the broader community strategies drawn up under the 2000 Act.

1.7   The recent White Papers, *Our Towns and Cities –The Future* and *Our Countryside – The Future*, and the National Strategy for Neighbourhood Renewal, set out our desire to see a more co-ordinated delivery of services. It will be important for housing authorities to take a more corporate approach to their housing services if these objectives are to be delivered. A more cross-cutting approach will also be necessary to ensure the success of local strategic partnerships. Equally, closer and better integrated working relations between housing, planning, health and social service authorities are essential to the successful delivery of many of the policies spelt out in this document, including for example, the delivery of affordable housing and the prevention of homelessness.

1.8   As Government we will play our part, providing the necessary support from the centre. In addition to annual guidance on authorities' Housing Investment Programmes and strategies, we published in August some best practice guidance on local housing needs assessment and updated guidance on stock surveys. Guidance is also available on producing housing strategies in rural areas.

1.9   The Housing Corporation will continue to develop its investment strategy in each region in close consultation with local authorities and other partners. Joint commissioning has proved an effective means of achieving collaborative working in a number of local authority areas, and the Corporation will be building on this in the future. We expect further development of joint commissioning to include programmes of schemes that meet identified needs across a number of local authorities. The Corporation is planning to publish good practice guidance on joint commissioning next year.

1.10   In addition, we are taking forward specific measures to strengthen local authorities' strategic role for housing and measures which will enhance the tools available to local authorities, for example to tackle low demand. Some of these were proposed in the Green Paper and include:

- giving local authorities greater discretion over private sector renewal. In particular we intend to legislate to give local authorities greater freedoms over grant conditions and repayment, renewal and repair;

- introducing a new system to assess whether housing meets acceptable health and safety standards, enabling more effective action to be taken where it does not;

- developing proposals for selective licensing of private landlords in low demand areas;

- introducing a single pot for local authority capital resources in 2002/03 to allow greater local discretion in spending decisions, building on the single pot for housing capital resources;

- giving local authorities greater flexibility and responsibility to ensure sustainable solutions for homeless people and to make better use of their own stock; and

- giving local authorities greater flexibility over lettings policies so that they can promote sustainable communities.

1.11   The following chapters of this statement explain in more detail how we are taking these proposals forward.

CHAPTER TWO

Encouraging sustainable home ownership

Our Key Measures are:

- To introduce legislation to improve and other measures the home buying and selling process

- To legislate to introduce commonhold and reform leasehold

- To introduce a Starter Home Initiative to help key workers to buy their own homes

- To help unemployed homeowners move into work through improvements to benefit support for mortgages

- To give local authorities greater flexibility in their support for private housing renovation

What the Green Paper said

2.1　Chapter 4 of the Green Paper set out our support for sustainable home ownership. This means a framework where owners can afford the commitments of ownership in the long term. The main contribution Government can make to sustainable home ownership is a robust economy in all parts of the country and a strong system of consumer protection. We are determined to avoid a return to the boom and bust economy of the past, which can erode the security many expect from their homes. And it creates an uncertain climate for investment – a house is the biggest investment most people make. In addition to existing proposals to improve the home buying and selling process, strengthen consumer protection, introduce a new tenure, commonhold, and reform leasehold law, the Green Paper put forward some new proposals for consultation. These included the Starter Home Initiative to help key workers into home ownership, additional help for unemployed home owners moving back into work and reforms to the way private sector renewal is funded.

What consultees said

2.2　A clear majority of those who commented on the Starter Home Initiative supported it, though many stressed that it should not be funded at the expense of other affordable housing programmes. Existing low cost home ownership (LCHO) schemes were thought to be suitable mechanisms for helping people on lower incomes to move into home ownership and to help in creating balanced communities. Some respondents considered that more flexibility within the current LCHO schemes would be desirable. Some respondents said that the Starter Home Initiative should support the provision of rented accommodation for key workers.

2.3   Respondents welcomed our proposals to improve the home buying and selling process with some commenting on the need to ensure the validity and reliability of the information contained in the 'seller's pack'. Our proposals to extend benefit help with mortgage payments and to introduce a four week benefit run-on for claimants who move into work, were widely welcomed. Respondents were keen to see a review of the grant and loan regimes for private sector renewal with a few reservations around loan giving powers for private repairs.

Our policy approach

2.4   We are taking forward all of the proposals in Chapter 4 of the Green Paper.

LOW COST HOME OWNERSHIP

2.5   We believe that current schemes supporting low cost home ownership provide a reasonable range of options for people on lower incomes who wish to achieve home ownership on a sustainable basis. We do, however, wish to encourage innovative approaches to support key workers through the Starter Home Initiative, described below. In addition, we will commission research into the operation and effectiveness of the existing Homebuy, conventional shared ownership and the Do-it-Yourself Shared Ownership (DIYSO) schemes. We will consider possible changes, including the longer term future of DIYSO, in the light of the research findings. In the meantime DIYSO will continue to be available as a local authority funded scheme at least until March 2002.

THE STARTER HOME INITIATIVE

2.6   We are going ahead with our proposals to introduce a Starter Home Initiative. In July we announced a significant budget for this programme – £250 million in total over the years 2001-02 to 2003-04. This is on top of increases to other housing programmes. We believe this should lay to rest concerns that the Starter Home Initiative would draw funding away from other programmes.

2.7   We expect the Starter Home Initiative will:

- provide help for around 10,000 key workers, particularly nurses, teachers and police, to buy their own homes in urban and rural areas where high prices would otherwise prevent them from living in or near the communities they serve;

- promote a culture of opportunity, choice and self-reliance and give people more of a stake in their housing and neighbourhoods;

- support other housing-related objectives which contribute to the regeneration or development of an area; and

- promote a better mix of housing tenures with the aim of achieving more sustainable mixed-income communities.

2.8 The Green Paper presented the Initiative in the context of our support for home ownership. We want to help people on the threshold of home ownership to achieve their aspirations. And this has wider benefits to society too. This rationale remains valid. For that reason, the funds earmarked for the Starter Home Initiative will be devoted to helping people who would not otherwise be able to afford home ownership.

2.9 We recognise that there is a need for a better supply of affordable rented accommodation, and that key workers will be among those needing such accommodation. Increased levels of housing investment through local authorities and the Housing Corporation will improve supply. We will also be asking local authorities to consider the housing needs of key workers – particularly nurses, teachers and the police – in their housing strategies which, in turn, influence the allocation of resources to housing schemes for particular groups. Together with better use of planning powers for affordable housing and new approaches to lettings policies, described later in this statement, these measures should increase the scope for letting affordable rented housing to key workers, especially where this helps to foster mixed and sustainable communities.

2.10 The distinction between the Starter Home Initiative and affordable rented accommodation will not be totally rigid. Schemes that promote shared ownership (involving part ownership, part renting of properties) will be eligible for funding under the Starter Home Initiative. Funding may also be used to support mixed tenure schemes, with the Starter Home Initiative subsidising low cost home ownership and other sources of funding providing rented homes.

2.11 In parallel with this statement the Department of the Environment, Transport and the Regions and the Housing Corporation are announcing details of how the Starter Home Initiative will operate. Scheme proposers, who could be from the public or private sector, will be invited to put forward proposals and compete for funding. We are aiming for a scheme that gives interested partners as much flexibility as possible to put in relevant and imaginative bids. Winning proposals will be announced and schemes commenced during 2001.

2.12   The key bidding criteria are given below:

STARTER HOME INITIATIVE

Schemes should:

- be targeted on groups of key workers amongst whom there are demonstrable recruitment and retention difficulties locally, whose services are essential to the local community, who must be located close to that community, and who would not otherwise be able to buy their own home;

- be targeted on urban or rural areas where house price affordability is a significant problem and where there is demonstrable excess demand for housing;

- normally be focused on homes in the bottom quartile of house prices in a local housing market and travel to work area;

- have low administrative costs per household helped, and demonstrate that "deadweight" costs are being kept to a minimum;

- have the support of the local authorities in whose areas they will be operating;

- demonstrate value for money;

- be possible under the current legislative framework.

Schemes could:

- contribute to other housing-related objectives (particularly promoting mixed tenure and sustainable communities, helping to regenerate deprived neighbourhoods, making use of empty property and redeveloping brownfield sites;

- involve repayable interest free equity loans, cash grants, or other innovative approaches which meet the main criteria above;

- cover housing market areas that span more than one local authority, provided that the proposals have the support of all the relevant authorities;

- provide added value to complement investment from the Starter Home Initiative (e.g. including funding from other sources, including employers of the key workers being targeted by the scheme).

Other requirements:

- where a home which has been purchased with an equity loan under the Starter Home Initiative is subsequently resold, some or all of any equity interest realised by the scheme manager should be recovered or recycled depending on the circumstances.

REFORM OF BENEFIT HELP WITH MORTGAGE INTEREST PAYMENTS

2.13 We are taking action to help unemployed home owners moving back into work. From 2001 new help will be available for homeowners moving off an income-related benefit into full-time work. Mortgage interest payments will continue for a further four weeks after starting work. This will ease the transition into work by providing more equal treatment between homeowners and those who rent. Around 60,000 homeowners are expected to benefit from this help each year with average gains of between £30 and £35 a week. In addition, benefit linking arrangements for homeowners taking up employment will be extended from the current 12 weeks to 52 weeks, so that if they have to reclaim benefit within one year they will automatically qualify for help with mortgage interest payments.

2.14 We have noted the concerns expressed by some respondents about possible longer term changes and, as set out in the Green Paper, will need to be satisfied that the suitability, coverage and take-up of mortgage payment protection insurance is sufficient to enable a better integrated public-private sector approach. We are not currently proposing any further changes to benefit help with mortgage interest payments beyond those described above to reduce disincentives to work. We will, however, keep the policy and the effectiveness of private insurance provision under review: in particular, we will monitor progress against the industry's target to increase take-up of mortgage payment protection insurance to 55% by 2004.

PRIVATE SECTOR RENEWAL

2.15 Privately owned homes make up the majority of homes in England. As we stated in the Green Paper we expect owner occupiers to maintain their homes from their own resources. But there are exceptions, such as cases where a household's income is inadequate to maintain their home or where the cumulative effect of a number of badly maintained houses reduces significantly the quality of the neighbourhood. In these circumstances some support from public money may be sensible. Our proposals build on the recommendations of the Urban Task Force which advocated the use of a wider range of policy tools to encourage private home improvements. Public investment in housing can play an important role in urban regeneration and will contribute to the proposals set out in the Urban White Paper for improving the physical fabric of our towns and cities.

2.16 We can achieve some of what we want without legislation. We are today issuing the first of a number of measures introducing new freedoms to declare renewal areas and group repair schemes and to give local authorities powers to waive the repayment of housing renewal grant in a range of circumstances. By putting in place these interim measures while we push ahead with the main body of reforms we hope to send a clear signal of our commitment not just to seeing these reforms through, but also of having them in place at the earliest opportunity.

2.17 From today, the minimum number of dwellings required in a renewal area is reduced from 300 to 50; both the proportion of private sector stock and the number of properties requiring works are reduced from three quarters to one third; the percentage of households on benefit are reduced from 30% to 10%. The minimum number of properties required for a group repair scheme is halved to two. They may include flats and need not contain a minimum percentage of unfit properties. And authorities may waive the requirement to repay grant where they are satisfied that it is reasonable to do so. These measures will enable local authorities to tackle areas of abandonment and help to stabilise areas of both private and public sector housing which are on the brink of decline or have suffered from low demand.

2.18   In the longer term, we are also proposing a major reform of existing legislation, details of which will be set out in a consultation paper to be issued shortly. Subject to the outcome of this consultation and Parliamentary approval we will introduce the reforms through a Regulatory Reform Order.

ASSISTANCE TO INDIVIDUAL HOMEOWNERS

2.19   The Green Paper proposed giving local authorities more discretion over how they give grants to individuals for home repairs and renovation. Proposals included broadening their loan-giving powers and giving them new powers to make payments to third parties to help lever in private finance for home improvement. Respondents supported additional flexibility within the existing grant structure, and most favoured the option of a general power. A number of respondents asked for additional powers, for example to be able to offer help with moving home as an alternative to improving or adapting someone's existing home.

2.20   In the light of this positive response, we intend to take our reform proposals a step further. We propose to introduce a new general power for local authorities to give financial assistance, or to provide labour and materials, for home improvement and repair. The new power would replace renovation grants, Houses in Multiple Occupation grants and common parts grants, home repair assistance and group repair. It would be subject to a minimal level of regulation. Local authorities would be able to choose between giving grants, loans or other forms of financial assistance such as loan guarantees, and to decide how much assistance to give and what conditions to attach. We will expect local authorities to set out their policies in their housing strategy. They can deliver these policies themselves or through other bodies, such as Home Improvement Agencies, for which we have provided additional financial support following the Spending Review. To ensure propriety, we will require authorities to publish their policy for giving assistance under their new power, and to have regard to the guidance we issue.

2.21   We want local authorities to make effective use of the full range of options at their disposal. We therefore propose to allow them to offer assistance under their general power to help people to buy another property where this is a better option than repairing or improving their existing home, or where demolition is the only answer to tackling low demand. This would replace the limited power currently available through relocation grants. In addition, local authorities would be able to offer a grant, loan or other assistance under their new powers to help disabled people with the cost of adapting their home or buying another property. This would not affect the statutory entitlement to a disabled facilities grant, which will remain unchanged.

AREA-BASED RENEWAL

2.22   As outlined above, we propose to enable local authorities to carry out works to groups of properties, as well as to individual homes, under their new general power. As there will no longer be a need for separate legislation to govern group repair, we intend to remove it. Similarly, we intend to remove the separate provisions governing relocation grants, which will be included within the new general power. This will give local authorities a wider range of options for dealing with poor condition housing and tackling low demand and would help support local clearance strategies.

2.23   We intend to retain the legislation governing renewal areas, which can play an important part in a comprehensive area-based regeneration strategy. As these provisions include powers of compulsion (powers to acquire land and powers of entry, for example) it will be necessary to retain the existing safeguards to protect the interest of local residents.

TACKLING LOW DEMAND IN THE PRIVATE SECTOR

2.24   Our policies will improve the toolkit available to tackle the problem of low demand in private sector housing. Low demand is a growing problem that affects all tenures and there is mounting concern at the damage it can inflict on neighbourhoods, often within a very short space of time. The causes of low demand are complex. They may differ according to area, and are taking time to understand. In preparation for the National Strategy for Neighbourhood Renewal, one of the Policy Action Teams, PAT 7, looked in depth at the issues and came up with nearly 40 recommendations at national, regional and local level. This has given us a valuable start in tackling the problems, and nearly every recommendation is being pursued. Some of those recommendations are progressed through the proposals set out in this statement. The action plan following up the National Strategy for Neighbourhood Renewal sets out in greater detail how the Government is addressing low demand. We are introducing today new freedoms into the existing legislation, which will give local authorities greater flexibility over grant conditions and repayment, renewal areas and group repair and give local authorities more tools to tackle low demand housing in the private sector.

REFORMING LEASEHOLD

2.25   The Housing Green Paper referred to our proposals for residential leasehold reform and the introduction of a new commonhold tenure for collective ownership and management of properties consisting of a number of units such as blocks of flats. We published for consultation in August a draft Commonhold and Leasehold reform Bill to implement these proposals. We will introduce a Bill, amended in the light of comments from consultees, as soon as Parliamentary time allows.

REFORMING THE HOME BUYING AND SELLING PROCESS

2.26   Our procedures for buying and selling homes are the slowest and most inefficient in Europe. Every year hundreds of thousands of people endure the misery of failed transactions, incurring often substantial abortive costs. Many people whose deals do go through have to wait an inordinate length of time.

2.27   Forty per cent of those who go through the process declare themselves dissatisfied with it. This is a damning statistic, and we are determined to do something about it. An efficient housing market benefits us all. We are pursuing a range of measures to increase certainty in the process and reduce delays. At the heart of our proposals is a Bill for the 2000/01 session to require sellers to prepare a "seller's pack" before marketing a property. This will ensure that the majority of potential problems are identified up front before consumers start incurring significant expenditure. The seller's pack will include a mid-level survey, carried out by an inspector certified by an independent body. The inspector will be liable to both buyer and seller. Provided the certification regime is fully operational, and subject to securing Parliamentary approval, we intend that these measures will take effect from 2003.

OTHER DEVELOPMENTS

2.28   The Department has set up a working group with the Council of Mortgage Lenders and others to review the potential benefits to consumers of securitisation in the mortgage market.

2.29   A consultation document was published by the Treasury on 26 October 2000, accompanying draft statutory instruments setting out the extent to which mortgages will be regulated by the Financial Services Authority and how financial promotions (advertisements) will be covered. Mortgage regulation should be introduced by early 2002.

2.30   A number of initiatives are being progressed to promote better performance in the construction industry. A Quality Mark scheme designed to protect against cowboy builders is being piloted in two areas in England.

2.31   The Government notes the broadly positive response to the idea of a repair cost index which was discussed in the Green Paper and is considering this further.

CHAPTER THREE

Promoting a healthy private rented sector

Our Key Measures are:

- To help well-intentioned landlords to improve their expertise through local authority accreditation schemes and other best practice initiatives

- To tackle the worst problems by introducing a compulsory licensing system for Houses in Multiple Occupation

- To develop proposals for selective licensing of other privately rented properties in areas of low demand

- To develop benefit measures to underpin our licensing proposals

- To continue to consider whether there are any tax measures which could make long-term investment in private rented housing a more attractive proposition

- To introduce a new health and safety rating scale for assessing the condition of homes in all tenures

What the Green Paper said

3.1   Chapter 5 of the Green Paper set out our objectives for securing a larger, better-quality, better-managed private rented sector. It proposed, or presented for discussion, a number of measures designed to:

- retain our many good and well-intentioned landlords, and help them to raise their standards further;

- persuade reputable investors to expand the supply of decent rented homes; and

- make the worst landlords perform better, or get out of the business altogether.

What consultees said

3.2   Consultees generally welcomed our objectives and overall approach. There was particularly strong support for publishing good practice guidance for local authorities on landlord accreditation schemes; for measures to raise standards in residential property management; for the introduction of a compulsory licensing scheme for Houses in Multiple Occupation; and for giving local authorities discretionary licensing powers for other private rented sector properties. There was some concern about the suggestion that, in areas of low housing demand, Housing Benefit, or the availability of direct payments of benefit to landlords, might be restricted where the landlord was providing poor standards or failing to control anti-social behaviour by tenants.

Our policy approach

RAISING THE STANDARDS OF GOOD AND WELL-INTENTIONED LANDLORDS

3.3   We will support good and well-intentioned landlords in a variety of ways. We will publish the results of research into voluntary landlord accreditation schemes and good practice guidance for landlords, in the spring of 2001. We are developing proposals for a scheme to provide low-cost management services for small landlords, in consultation with landlord associations, the Housing Corporation and registered social landlords. We are working with the relevant trade bodies to develop the National Approved Lettings Scheme (NALS) further so as to provide independent quality assurance for all lettings agents. The pilot Tenancy Deposit Scheme (TDS), which aims to provide security for tenants' deposits and independent resolution of disputes, is now under way in a number of selected areas around the country. We will evaluate the progress and success of NALS and TDS carefully and consider in the light of the results whether more formal action is required. All of these measures will help to raise standards in the private rented sector, benefiting responsible landlords and tenants.

PERSUADING REPUTABLE INVESTORS TO EXPAND THE SUPPLY OF PRIVATE RENTED HOUSING

3.4   In the Green Paper we mentioned perceptions of difficulty in getting quick and certain redress through the courts against defaulting tenants as one factor inhibiting more investment in the sector. The Lord Chancellor has consulted on proposals for reform of housing and land civil court procedures, and the Civil Procedure Rule Committee is considering proposed new rules. The Lord Chancellor's review of civil enforcement has concluded that service standards should be introduced to the courts, setting a target for evictions to be carried out no later than four weeks after the bailiff first receives the warrant.

3.5   We will continue to consider whether there are any tax measures, consistent with overall fiscal policy, which could make long-term investment in decent quality private rented housing a more attractive proposition.

3.6   Empty homes and vacant space above shops can provide an important source of additional rented accommodation. The Urban and Rural White Papers contain measures to promote regeneration in our urban and rural areas by encouraging re-use of empty and under used properties. Local authorities and others are already doing a lot to bring empty properties back into use, particularly in areas of low demand. We are taking further action to encourage them to develop comprehensive empty property strategies and requiring them to report progress annually. We have also announced plans to introduce two new fiscal incentives. These are a 100% capital allowance for creating flats over shops for letting; and reform of VAT to encourage additional conversion of properties for residential use.

MAKING THE WORST LANDLORDS BETTER

SELECTIVE LICENSING OF PRIVATE LANDLORDS

3.7   Neighbourhoods suffering from low demand can be further destabilised by the actions of unscrupulous and criminal landlords. We will therefore consult on proposals for selective licensing of private landlords in areas of low demand. The objective will be to raise the standard of the private rented stock or management in the most deprived areas and tackle abuse, and in some cases, large-scale criminal activity by certain landlords and their tenants which has been undermining the local community in parts of our cities. Each scheme would be subject to individual approval by the Secretary of State. We would only countenance such schemes in areas where tenants could find readily available alternative accommodation should the landlord fail to obtain, or lose, a licence or withdraw from the market. We aim to consult on proposals for legislation in the spring of 2001.

HMO LICENSING

3.8   Physical conditions and management standards are often at their worst in houses in multiple occupation (HMOs). We remain committed to introducing a compulsory licensing system for HMOs. It has not proved possible to find legislative time in this Parliamentary session, but HMO licensing remains a commitment for the Government and legislation will be introduced as soon as Parliamentary time allows. Property condition will be a key criterion in any licensing scheme. We will make use of the time before introduction of an HMO Licensing Bill to refine our proposals to replace the fitness standard with a regime based on the new Housing Health and Safety Rating System.

HOUSING HEALTH AND SAFETY RATING SYSTEM

3.9   The current basis for assessing property condition is the fitness standard, set out in its most recent form in the Local Government and Housing Act 1989. There is a consensus that the fitness standard does not reflect a modern understanding of the health and safety risks inherent in property condition. The Government has therefore been developing a new, evidence-based system for rating the severity of hazards in the home, the Housing Health and Safety Rating System. We published in July guidance for local authorities on the operation of the new system, which we intend will become the new tool for judging whether property conditions are acceptable. Local authorities' powers and duties to secure decent housing conditions need to be overhauled to enable them to make the most effective use of the rating system and we will publish proposals for consultation shortly. In the meantime, we are encouraging authorities to familiarise themselves with the new system by using it informally alongside the fitness standard.

HOUSING BENEFIT CONDITIONALITY

3.10   In the Green Paper, we put forward for consideration a number of suggestions for using restrictions on Housing Benefit, or its direct payment to landlords. Our aim would be to encourage the less reputable landlords to improve the state of their stock and its management and to tackle problems of anti-social behaviour by their tenants. Some consultees expressed reservations, including whether the measures would complicate the rules and therefore increase local authorities' difficulties in administering the scheme.

3.11   We recognise the concerns that some have raised. However, we remain concerned about the abuse of the benefit system by unscrupulous landlords who provide poor standards of accommodation and about anti-social behaviour amongst some tenants. We believe that abuses can be tackled in ways that will avoid any difficulties envisaged by consultees. We will therefore develop benefit measures linked to our proposals for mandatory HMO licensing and selective licensing of private landlords. We believe that restricting Housing Benefit, or its direct payment to landlords, will prove an effective way to underpin a licensing regime in low demand areas and target the worst landlords.

CHAPTER FOUR

Raising the quality of social housing

Our Key Measures are:

- To bring all social housing up to a decent standard by 2010 supported by additional resources

- To ensure that local authorities adopt a more business-like approach to housing management and investment

- To support the transfer of up to 200,000 homes each year from local authorities to registered social landlords where tenants vote for it

- To encourage local authorities to set up new arms length management arrangements for council housing, with additional investment opportunities

- To promote and fund new Private Finance Initiative schemes to improve council housing

- To ensure the consistent and rigorous application of Best Value and Tenant Participation Compacts across all social housing

What the Green Paper said

4.1 Chapter 7 of the Green Paper set out our strategy to improve the quality of social housing and our commitment to bring all social housing up to a decent standard within a decade. Our strategy included additional investment for local authorities to tackle the £19 billion backlog of renovation and improvements, along with a new financial framework for more efficient investment in stock maintenance. In addition, other approaches were proposed including: an increased stock transfer programme; a new option for strong performing local authorities to move their stock management into arms length arrangements and gain access to additional borrowing; and the Private Finance Initiative schemes. The Green Paper made clear that Best Value and Tenant Participation Compact principles have a key role to play and that they need to be rigorously applied to help raise standards for all social tenants.

What consultees said

4.2 There was a broad welcome for the Government's recognition of the size of the repairs backlog, the need for increased funding and the commitment to bring all social housing up to a decent standard within a decade. Half of those who commented on the proposals to encourage more authorities to consider the benefits of stock transfer agreed that it was the way forward. A significant number of respondents made the point that transfer is just one option: local discretion and tenant choice are important considerations. Some raised concerns that stock transfer was being given greater Government support than other options and that this impeded the level of real choice available to local authorities and their tenants. Subject to seeing further details, four fifths of those who commented on the proposals for arms length companies welcomed them and the increased choice this would give local authorities and their tenants. Some respondents felt that insufficient weight had been given to ethnic and equality issues. There was strong support for emphasis on the principles of Best Value and tenant participation, and agreement that registered social landlords should be subject to an inspection regime similar to that for local authorities.

Our policy approach

4.3   We have responded positively to concerns about the level of resources. Our spending plans up to 2004, announced in July, provide the necessary resources to reduce by one third the number of homes in the social sector that currently fail to meet the set standard of decency. This will set us well on the road to meeting our target that all social housing should be decent within a decade.

4.4   In line with our National Strategy for Neighbourhood Renewal, most of the improvements will take place in the most deprived areas. Decent housing gives people a stronger sense of identity and security and is an important part of our wider strategy for building more sustainable communities in urban and rural areas.

4.5   We believe that a local authority is best placed to perform its housing responsibilities effectively where its strategic functions are separated from its management functions, even if it retains ownership. Our proposals represent a balanced programme to deliver real improvement in quality; promote a more diverse range of social landlords; and give tenants more of a say in how, and by whom, their housing is managed.

4.6   Local authorities will have a range of options available to them to improve the quality of social housing. A **new financial framework** is being introduced, including detailed guidance on business planning, collecting and managing stock information and local housing needs assessment. This provides local authorities and their tenants with all the tools necessary to identify the appropriate options and make sound, long term business decisions. Any of the options might apply to all, or to a part of, their stock, but whichever route they propose to take, the principles of Best Value and tenant participation should be paramount.

4.7   There are four choices available to authorities and their tenants. Under the first three the housing stock remains in local authority ownership.

(i)   Use the authority's own resources and those made available through the new Major Repairs Allowance and credit approvals to maintain and improve the stock in the most efficient way consistent with the new financial framework, Best Value and the recommendations of the Construction Task Force.

(ii)   Set up arms length arrangements. An extra £460 million over three years has been made available for investment in local authority owned housing, for authorities which have set up arms-length arrangements, demonstrated excellence in their performance under the new Best Value regime and met certain other criteria.

(iii)   Pursue PFI (Private Finance Initiative) schemes. Funding to support an extra £600 million of PFI investment will be made available for housing schemes in the period 2002/03 to 2003/04.

(iv) Transfer stock to registered social landlords. We will support the transfer of up to 200,000 homes a year if local authorities and tenants so choose.

LOCAL AUTHORITY RETAINED STOCK

4.8   For local authorities which retain ownership and management of their housing in the short or long term, the new financial framework will provide for proper asset management and investment within their Housing Revenue Accounts. One of the changes being made is the introduction of a new Major Repairs Allowance (MRA) to be paid as part of Housing Revenue Account subsidy. The MRA reflects the resources necessary to maintain the condition of the stock in the medium term. The allowance, which will be financed by earmarking part of the resources previously provided as credit approvals, will be £1.6 billion in 2001/02, with the amount per dwelling increased in line with inflation in the subsequent two years.

4.9   We are also increasing management allowances in line with the recommendations of the National Strategy for Neighbourhood Renewal about the importance of on the spot delivery of services. This reflects the findings of the Social Exclusion Unit's Policy Action Team 5 on housing management that a good housing management service with a local presence can make a positive contribution to reducing social exclusion.

4.10   Most local authorities will also continue to have access to housing basic credit approvals as well as their own resources (capital receipts and revenue contributions to capital expenditure). Under the Government's new spending plans, housing credit approvals are set to rise from £705 million in 2001/02 to £842 million by 2003/04. This increase is in addition to funding for the new Major Repairs Allowance and the extra investment through arms length arrangements.

ARMS-LENGTH ARRANGEMENTS

4.11   Our new spending plans include extra investment of £160 million in 2002/03 and £300 million in 2003/04. These sums will be available in the form of borrowing for authorities that have retained their stock and established arms-length arrangements to manage all or part of it and which have demonstrated excellence in the delivery of services to their tenants. We expect the investment to improve nearly 100,000 local authority homes by 2003/04. We have been discussing the details of how this option might work with the local authority associations and others. A consultation paper on this proposal is being published today.

PRIVATE FINANCE INITIATIVE (PFI)

4.12   Eight local authorities are already taking part in pathfinder PFI schemes to improve their tenants' housing. Next year, we are providing resources to enable £160 million of investment through those pathfinder schemes. We are developing an evaluation framework ensuring early lessons from the pathfinders are picked up and longer term monitoring is put in place. We will be providing additional resources for £300 million of investment in 2002/03 and a further £300 million in 2003/04 to enable more authorities to implement PFI schemes. Bids have recently been invited for new PFI housing schemes for 2002/03.

HOUSING STOCK TRANSFER

4.13   Following the Spending Review we made available resources sufficient to fund the transfer of up to 200,000 homes in each of the next three years from local authorities to registered social landlords. We will continue our policy of support for stock transfer where the local authority selects that option and has the support of tenants. We will make a one-off payment to meet the housing debt where it exceeds the local authority's capital receipt, but we will not cover the costs of early debt redemption premiums. These must be met by the transfer receipt or by other resources from the local authority if the transfer is to go ahead.

4.14   As foreshadowed in the Green Paper, we are feeding into the transfer guidance results of our review of the transfer process. There are several main strands to this.

INCREASING COMPETITION FOR THE SUCCESSOR LANDLORD, AND FOR FUNDING

4.15   Our aim is to ensure tenants have a genuine choice of successor landlord. The guidance for applicants for the 2001 transfer programme includes strengthened material on choosing a successor landlord, requiring evidence that tenants have been given a choice of landlord, including existing and new registered social landlords, to receive the transferring stock. We are now giving more detailed consideration to a number of key issues to help establish the best way forward, aiming to finish this work early in 2001 so that a number of local authorities could pilot a yet more competitive approach in the 2002 transfer programme. We also want to maximise the return that transfer delivers to the local authority and the taxpayer and so we are also actively engaged, with the Housing Corporation, on work aimed at widening the pool of funders.

GROUP STRUCTURES

4.16   The Guidance for 2001 programme applicants outlines the key areas for consideration when setting up group structures. A group structure is an arrangement of associated registered social landlords operating as subsidiaries of a parent organisation. The arrangement needs to provide for each registered social landlord to secure independence from the group, although in practice this is unlikely to take place in the early years after the transfer. These have been developed in the light of recent experience of whole transfers of urban stock (Tameside and Coventry) in which the local authorities' stock was transferred to subsidiary registered social landlords within a group structure. That experience included considering a range of issues (for example ownership, operational independence and de-merger) about how groups should be structured and how they operate. We are continuing to develop ideas with the Housing Corporation, with a view to publishing further guidance.

TENANT PARTICIPATION

4.17   In the light of research, we have issued revised guidelines on improving local authorities' consultation documents and we will publish shortly guidance about the role of the Independent Tenant Adviser (ITA). This guidance should help tenants, local authorities and ITAs to understand the dimensions of the ITA role, and to get the best out of the process. Moreover, in evaluating Best Value in housing and Tenant Participation Compacts, we are exploring examples of good practice in involving tenants in business planning and deciding on the options for their areas. We expect valuable lessons to emerge from this study which could be applied more widely in the stock transfer context. Depending on the outcome, we will consider whether more work is needed to draw out further lessons on tenant participation specifically for stock transfers.

ADDRESSING THE INTERESTS OF BLACK AND MINORITY ETHNIC COMMUNITIES

4.18   The transfer programme provides an opportunity for greater participation in the ownership and management of social housing stock. Our new guidance requires authorities to consider the needs of black and minority ethnic communities and the role of existing black and minority ethnic registered social landlords when contemplating transfer. This is echoed by our annual Housing Investment Programme guidance to local authorities, which requires local authorities to take account of the needs and aspirations of black and minority ethnic people and communities in their areas when drawing up their housing strategies.

COMMUNITY HOUSING TASK FORCE

4.19   We are also establishing a Community Housing Task Force from April next year to assist local authorities, tenants and potential social landlords to achieve successful transfers – transfers that empower tenants and yield substantial improvements in the social housing stock by attracting new management skills and sources of funds.

4.20   The services of the Task Force will be available to an authority and its tenants once the authority has concluded that it is interested in pursuing stock transfer. Prior to that stage the Chartered Institute of Housing and the Local Government Association have set up a new advisory service, called Choice for Housing, to assist the process.

BEST VALUE AND TENANT PARTICIPATION

4.21   Whichever option local authorities and their tenants choose to pursue, those managing social housing stock will need to ensure improvements in housing management and effective tenant empowerment, through Best Value and Tenant Participation Compact principles.

4.22   The central purpose of Best Value is to make a real and positive difference to services which local people receive. In housing, Best Value will ensure that tenants and residents are actively involved in the planning and delivery of housing services. They will be involved in the Best Value Reviews of services and in the monitoring of performance targets set out in the annual Best Value Performance Plans.

4.23   The housing reviews and Inspection regime under-pinning Best Value should act as a catalyst for continuous improvement in local authority housing services. The Housing Inspectorate began its first inspections at the end of July 2000 and published its first reports in September. More than 30 housing authorities will have been inspected by the end of the 2000 calendar year, and a further 80 inspections will have taken place by April 2001.

4.24   The success of the Housing Inspectorate will be judged by its ability to recognise good performance as well as bad, to promote excellence as well as taking those providing poor services to task. Above all, its role is to help local housing authorities provide high quality services, within their available resources, in response to the aspirations of their communities.

4.25   As well as directly employing inspectors and, over the course of time, commissioning external inspectors, the Inspectorate also intends to draw on the service-expertise of current local authority officers and other professionals through a limited programme of secondments, some of which would be on a mutual basis. A programme of recruitment and training of Tenant Advisers to play an active part in appropriate housing inspections has also begun.

4.26   The Housing Corporation is also embracing its new objective to promote the improved performance of registered social landlords. Best Value will become integral to the Corporation's and registered social landlords' activities in a parallel fashion to that being adopted by local authorities.

4.27   The Housing Corporation is placing a strong emphasis on registered social landlords drawing up and working to local performance plans, in consultation with their tenants. The Corporation is currently reviewing performance standard expectations of registered social landlords – changing the emphasis away from detailed prescription towards a focus on key outcomes. The Corporation proposes setting out a code derived from its new regulatory mandate. This will set out the principles it expects registered social landlords to adhere to when carrying out their business with an emphasis on Best Value outcomes and a culture of continuous improvement.

4.28   At the same time the Corporation is developing its new inspection regime to focus on service standards provided to tenants and customers.

4.29   The Corporation has recently published a policy document, 'Communities in Control', setting out a framework to encourage tenant participation in the running of their communities. This is supported by a new Community Training and Enabling grant programme to provide financial support enabling RSL tenants to explore the community housing options open to them. Grant funding of £11 million will be made available through this programme over the next three years.

4.30   Local Tenant Participation Compacts should be based upon the National Framework for Tenant Participation Compacts published in June 1999. For tenants, drawing up and signing a local compact is a major step forward in ensuring they can work together with their council to develop a shared vision for their area, by planning what they want to see changed or improved and agreeing how it will be done. Under compacts all tenants should have the opportunity to influence housing decisions which affect them and their community. They should also be able to choose a level of involvement that they want. In addition, Compacts will also ensure that tenants have the support they need to help them take part effectively, including access to training, facilities and advice. However the framework offers a non prescriptive approach giving councils and tenants the flexibility needed for them to develop their compacts to meet the local priorities and circumstances whether they live in urban or rural communities. We also want tenants to have the opportunities for greater control of housing and housing services where they want this and we will be looking at how to improve existing procedures to smooth the way for tenants.

CHAPTER FIVE

Providing new affordable housing

Our Key Measures are:

- To more than double investment in affordable housing over the next three years

- To encourage the strategic allocation of Housing Corporation funding to match regional and local priorities

- To apply the Construction Task Force's recommendations and new construction techniques to Housing Corporation-funded developments to improve efficiency, design and quality

- To produce best practice guidance for local authorities to encourage more effective use of planning powers to provide affordable housing within private developments

---

What the Green Paper said

5.1   Chapter 8 of the Green Paper set out our approach to the delivery of new affordable housing in line with local needs. It suggested that decisions on new housing provision should be based on an assessment of needs and priorities at regional and local levels, through the development of regional housing statements, local housing strategies and local plans. The chapter outlined the current mechanisms for delivering affordable housing through the Housing Corporation's Approved Development Programme, Local Authority Social Housing Grant and the planning system. Ways of enhancing the delivery of affordable housing through these mechanisms to improve quality and choice and promote more sustainable communities were also set out in the Green Paper.

What consultees said

5.2   There was broad support for the overall approach set out in the Green Paper although some respondents considered that extra public funding was required to meet current and projected housing needs. A majority of those commenting on the proposed development of a more flexible approach to the allocation of Housing Corporation funding based on priorities identified in Regional Housing Statements, agreed that this was a sensible way forward. There was also support for the proposal that a forward looking indicator of the prospective growth in demand for social housing should be included in the Housing Needs Index which will continue to be used to allocate Housing Corporation funding between regions. A significant number of respondents commented that the grant rates for social housing investment needed to be reviewed, particularly to reflect proposed changes in policy on rents. There was support for giving greater encouragement to the development of mixed communities through both housing and planning policies. Many respondents also welcomed the commitment to produce good practice guidance for local authorities on the use of planning powers to deliver affordable housing although some commented that these powers needed to be strengthened.

Our policy approach

5.3 We believe that the approach set out in the Green Paper remains appropriate and welcome the support for it. We recognise that in many areas there is a need for more affordable housing. And that there is a need for better integration of social and private sector housing to promote sustainable communities. We do not believe that either national or regional estimates of need can adequately reflect the diversity of needs and priorities which exist at the local level. Local authorities are best placed to carry out assessments of housing need in their area. In areas of low demand for housing, we will expect any public investment in new housing to form part of a regeneration programme that addresses the underlying problems and ensures that housing investment is not wasted by providing new housing where there is an oversupply. We set out below the way in which we are taking forward some of the key issues following consultation.

PROVISION OF FUNDING

5.4 Following the Spending Review, we have increased significantly the resources available to fund new affordable housing. The Housing Corporation's Approved Development Programme (ADP) has been increased by £50m to £687m this year (2000/01) and will rise to £1,236m by 2003/04, nearly doubling the programme. To reflect increases in scheme costs and the proposed move to a new rent regime for registered social landlords (who provide most new affordable housing) we have increased the headline grant rate from 54% this year to 60% for the 2001/02 ADP. The Housing Corporation is also carrying out a detailed review of the grant rate framework to take account of the proposed changes in rent structures set out in this document and to help alleviate the problems currently experienced in implementing new developments in some areas. The Corporation aims to make recommendations to Ministers by spring 2001 in time for any changes to be introduced for 2002/03.

5.5 In addition to the extra ADP funding we are also providing £250 million of new investment over the next three years to assist key workers to buy their own homes in areas of relatively high house prices through the Starter Home Initiative, described earlier in this statement. The extra funding through the ADP, together with the Starter Home Initiative, demonstrates the Government's commitment to the provision of affordable housing to meet future needs.

5.6 In parallel with this increase in resources the Housing Corporation is continuing to implement the changes described in the Green Paper to help ensure that the money is better targeted to meet priority needs.

5.7 The Corporation is continuing the process of reducing reliance on the Housing Needs Index (HNI) for the allocation of resources to local authority areas. For 2001/02 the Corporation aims to increase the proportion of funding allocated on the basis of strategic priorities to around 50% in all regions apart from London where a figure of 40% is proposed. Subject to continuing progress with the development of regional housing statements, and broad consensus on the investment priorities emerging from them, the Corporation is aiming to move away entirely from the use of the HNI within all regions by 2003/04.

5.8　The Corporation is taking forward other measures to improve the targeting and delivery of the ADP. These include: closer monitoring of the extent to which schemes support the development of mixed communities; evaluation of the five pilot acquisition and demolition schemes in the North West and North East; and support for a number of pilot Housing Regeneration Companies which will co-ordinate regeneration programmes within housing areas at risk of decline, supporting proposals in our National Strategy for Neighbourhood Renewal. We will consider further development of these initiatives in support of our wider regeneration objectives in the light of the pilots. In addition, in order to address demand and sustainability issues, the Corporation has recently introduced a sustainability toolkit for use by registered social landlords when considering new housing investment funded through the ADP. This will help ensure that the long term demand for housing in an area is properly considered and that investment is not wasted in places that do not have a long term future.

5.9　We wish to see registered social landlords' development programmes incorporating the recommendations of the Construction Task Force to increase the speed and quality of construction projects while reducing their cost. The Corporation is continuing to take forward this agenda. Registered social landlords are being encouraged, through the ADP bidding process, to adopt processes for continuous measurement and re-evaluation of their performance in construction procurement. The Corporation has also developed a special programme within the ADP to encourage the greater use of pre-assembly and off-site manufacturing techniques. Further details are provided in the Corporation's National Investment Strategy for 2001/02. We also expect to see quality improvements through the introduction of Housing Quality Indicators which will allow schemes to be evaluated on the basis of quality rather than simply of cost.

LOCAL AUTHORITIES' ROLE

5.10　The Green Paper also noted that local authorities have a key role in the planning and delivery of affordable housing within their areas. In July, following the Spending Review, we announced an increase in housing capital resources to be made available to local authorities for the three years 2001/02 to 2003/04. This followed the substantial extra resources provided following the 1998 Comprehensive Spending Review. This will give local authorities greater scope to fund, through Local Authority Social Housing Grant, the provision of new affordable housing in areas where there are currently significant shortages.

5.11　Local authorities also have significant opportunities to secure an element of affordable housing within new housing developments through the planning process. The policy is set out in "Planning Policy Guidance Note 3: Housing" and in Circular 6/98. Although some respondents expressed concerns about the effectiveness of this process, we believe that the current policy already gives local authorities sufficient powers to deliver affordable housing through the planning system. The key requirement is for local authorities to make effective use of these powers. We are therefore researching how local planning authorities are implementing the policy at present. We expect to produce good practice guidance next year.

5.12　Local housing needs assessments underpin policies for the delivery of affordable housing. We have recently published guidance to help local authorities produce these assessments. We are monitoring more closely how local authorities develop and implement their policies for delivering affordable housing. This is being done through the Housing Investment Programme (HIP) process. In particular we will collect data on the amount of affordable housing provided under planning agreements.

AFFORDABLE HOUSING IN RURAL AREAS

5.13   The Green Paper emphasised that local housing strategies must recognise the needs of rural communities. In many rural areas local people can find themselves priced out of the local housing market. Our strategy for delivering more affordable housing in rural areas is set out in our recently published Rural White Paper, 'Our Countryside – The Future'. But we summarise here the key elements of housing policy that will benefit rural areas.

- The Housing Corporation's rural programme funds new affordable housing in settlements with less than 3,000 inhabitants. Over the next three years we will double the number of approvals for affordable homes provided through the rural programme. The proportion of dwellings approved by the Corporation will increase from the current target of 3.4% of the ADP to a new target of 6.4%.

- We expect the number of affordable homes provided through the ADP in larger rural communities and market towns to increase, as a result of the extra funding being made available over the next three years.

- We expect local authorities to increase their funding for affordable housing through Local Authority Social Housing Grant in rural areas where there is high demand.

- We will ensure funding for the new Starter Home Initiative is available to support low cost home ownership in rural as well as urban areas, where this meets the needs of key workers and the communities they serve.

- We expect local authorities to make greater and more effective use of their planning powers to provide more affordable housing in rural areas.

CHAPTER SIX

Promoting choice through lettings in social housing

> **Our Key Measures are:**
> - To legislate to facilitate more choice-based lettings approaches
> - To support and evaluate pilot schemes to test choice-based lettings approaches
> - To promote choice-based lettings approaches more generally

What the Green Paper said

6.1 In Chapter 9 of the Green Paper, we said that social landlords should consider themselves providers of a lettings service, responsive to the needs and wishes of individuals, rather than as housing allocators. By offering choice landlords will empower tenants to create sustainable communities and make the best use of the nation's housing stock. Specific proposals included: encouraging cross boundary and cross tenure applications; removing the power to impose blanket restrictions preventing groups of people from applying for social housing; and the development of local lettings policies to help create sustainable communities.

What respondents said

6.2 The principle of choice in lettings was broadly welcomed by respondents across the country. Many respondents highlighted the practical difficulties of offering choice in high demand areas where demand exceeds supply and said that a balance was needed between need and choice.

6.3 It was recognised that cross boundary and cross tenure applications were desirable and required practical joint working between landlords. The vast majority (80%) of respondents, who expressed an opinion, agreed with the proposal to remove blanket exclusions. A range of respondents from all areas supported local lettings policies, but with a recognition that they needed to involve local people, and be reviewed and monitored.

Our policy approach

6.4 We remain firmly of the view, set out in the Green Paper, that greater choice for tenants should be incorporated wherever possible into lettings policies for social housing, while continuing to meet housing need. We believe that if people are able to have a greater say about where they live this will help to create sustainable communities. By widening the scope for movement across local authority boundaries and between local authorities and registered social landlords, we can make better use of the national housing stock. But we do not want to be prescriptive about the approach adopted. We believe the right way forward is for local authorities and registered social landlords to decide in the light of local circumstances, and drawing on the experience of the pilot studies, the ways in which they should amend or develop their existing arrangements.

6.5   We have announced a new fund (£11m over three years from April 2001) to support pilot schemes which test choice-based approaches to lettings policies. We will be looking to support a range of innovative pilots with a strong emphasis on partnership working between and across local authorities, registered social landlords and other stakeholders. We shall also want to test what works in different situations, such as in areas of high and low demand. Together these will enable a variety of choice-based approaches to be tested. We will be announcing the successful pilots early in 2001. The pilots will be evaluated closely. There will be regular dissemination of lessons learnt and we will promote successful approaches through good practice guidance.

6.6   Whilst we accept that it is not easy to incorporate more choice in areas of high demand, we do not accept that improvements cannot be brought about with commitment and imagination. Moreover, we believe the improvements to the supply of affordable housing that will result from our new spending plans will help ease the problems in high demand areas and make it somewhat easier for social landlords to offer a greater degree of choice to new and existing tenants.

6.7   Lettings policies will need to be sensitive to the problems which can arise where there is a concentration of poor and vulnerable households within an area of social deprivation, and the need to promote more sustainable communities. This can be particularly important in education, where schools are dealing with multiple social and economic challenges. We shall encourage housing departments to consult with local education departments (or with the local education authority in non-unitary areas) about the impact of lettings policies in areas of deprivation, where these include schools that fall within the Government's categories of schools requiring special help or support.

6.8   We do not believe that the lettings policy of any one social housing provider in an area should be managed in isolation. Rather, local authorities and registered social landlords should consider jointly the best approach to be pursued, if the best use is to be made of the stock and tenants are to receive the best possible service. For that reason we intend to strengthen the obligation on registered social landlords to work with local authorities on lettings.

6.9   We are introducing legislation in the 2000/01 Parliamentary session to remove the scope to impose blanket restrictions preventing groups of people from applying for social housing. Legislation will facilitate choice-based lettings approaches, in particular, through:

- removal of the requirement for local housing authorities to maintain a housing register;

- a right for existing and aspirate tenants to apply for housing accommodation, subject to certain exceptions;

- allowing local authorities greater discretion to determine lettings policies appropriate to their localities while continuing to meet housing need.

CHAPTER SEVEN

Strengthening the protection available to the homeless

> **Our Key Measures are:**
>
> - To legislate to place a stronger duty on local housing authorities to accommodate people who are homeless through no fault of their own and who are in priority need
>
> - To extend the groups of vulnerable homeless people who have a priority need for accommodation
>
> - To legislate to give housing authorities the power to provide accommodation for people who are homeless through no fault of their own but do not have priority need, where there is suitable available housing
>
> - To legislate to require housing authorities to take a multi-agency strategic approach to tackling homelessness

What the Green paper said

7.1 Chapter 9 of the Green Paper detailed our proposals to improve the protection for priority need households who become homeless through no fault of their own.

7.2 The proposals included strengthening the main homelessness duty by removing the obligation on authorities to consider whether other accommodation was available and removing the two year limitation on the duty itself. Other proposals included:

- requiring local authorities to take a multi-agency strategic approach to preventing and responding to homelessness;

- encouraging authorities to offer homeless applicants a choice of settled accommodation;

- widening the homelessness safety net by introducing additional priority need categories and removing the two year restriction on the use of the local authority's own housing stock; and

- giving authorities a new power to provide temporary accommodation for non-priority need homeless applicants.

What respondents said

7.3 There was almost unanimous support, from those who responded, for the homelessness proposals. Only five respondents specifically opposed them.

7.4   A number of respondents considered that additional resources would be necessary to implement these proposals and to adopt a strategic approach to homelessness.

Our Proposals

7.5   We are determined to provide stronger support for people who become unintentionally homeless. In taking forward our proposals, we will extend the priority need categories of homeless people to include 16 and 17 year olds; care leavers aged 18-21; and applicants who are vulnerable as a result of an institutionalised background or as a result of fleeing domestic violence or harassment. We will make these changes shortly by Order under section 189 of the Housing Act 1996. We will issue statutory guidance about these changes.

7.6   We are introducing legislation in the 2000/01 Parliamentary session to make a number of changes to the existing homelessness legislation. These will include strengthening the main homelessness duty in a number of ways. We will repeal the current two year limitation that applies to the duty and require local housing authorities to secure suitable accommodation for all applicants who are unintentionally homeless and in priority need until a settled housing solution is found. Authorities will be expected to offer some choice of settled accommodation before bringing a duty to an end. We will also repeal the requirement to consider whether other suitable accommodation is available before an authority can let its own housing to a homeless household, and the two year restriction on the use of local authority stock to provide housing.

7.7   We will strengthen the safety net for unintentionally homeless applicants who are not in priority need by giving housing authorities a new power to secure accommodation for this client group, where resources permit.

7.8   We also want local authorities to take a more strategic approach to the prevention of homelessness. We will include in our legislation a requirement that local authorities undertake reviews of homelessness and formulate effective strategies on the back of those, in consultation with other organisations working to prevent homelessness or provide support for vulnerable people in their area. Strategies will be informed by the reviews which will consider all homelessness groups in the district and the provision available to meet their needs. They will need to be integrated with local housing strategies. A more multi-agency strategic approach will help authorities address and tackle problems of homelessness effectively. Clearly this is vital in areas where homelessness is a widespread problem. But we consider the benefits from taking a multi-agency strategic approach are such that they should apply to all local housing authorities.

7.9   A revised Code of Guidance will be prepared to reflect these changes and to make it easier for local authorities to follow and identify the key statutory requirements. We are also commissioning research on local authorities' responses to homelessness strategies from which good practice guidance will be produced alongside the revised Code.

7.10   We will provide local authorities with additional revenue funding of £8 million each year to meet the additional costs these proposals will incur.

7.11   In advance of the legislative reform we strongly urge local authorities to adopt a more multi-agency strategic approach to tackling homelessness.

CHAPTER EIGHT

New forms of tenure for social housing

Our Key Measures are:

- To consider a single form of tenure for social tenancies
- To consider more flexible forms of tenure to enable social landlords to make better use of their stock

---

What the Green Paper said

8.1 Chapter 9 of the Green Paper confirmed our belief that the security of tenure enjoyed by social housing tenants should not be reduced. It signalled our intention to look at the benefits and options for a new single form of tenure for the social rented sector and also at creating new flexibilities for landlords to make better use of their stock.

What consultees said

8.2 A relatively small number of respondents to the Green Paper commented on these proposals. Of those who did, the majority, ranging from housing providers to tenant organisations, were supportive of the principle of a single form of tenure. However, they registered concerns about how the Right to Buy would be affected and were keen to ensure that security of tenure in social housing was not eroded. Fewer people commented on more flexible forms of tenure. Of those who did, the majority offered support where they believed new forms of tenure could encourage diversity, stability and choice within a community. Emphasis was placed on the need for any new systems to be backed up by tough guidance and regulation.

Our policy approach

8.3 The responses confirmed our view that a single form of tenure for social housing tenants is desirable and is likely to be welcomed. But we recognise that there are a number of issues that still need to be resolved, and will work with representative bodies, such as the Local Government Association, the Chartered Institute of Housing, the National Housing Federation, Shelter and tenant representative groups on detailed proposals for further consultation.

8.4 Similarly, the response to more flexible forms of tenure indicates that further work on this would be welcomed and we propose to set this in train in discussion with interested parties.

8.5 In taking these ideas forward, we will liaise closely with the Scottish Executive, who are already well advanced in preparing to introduce provision for a single form of tenure for social housing. As we said in the Green Paper, we do not propose any significant change to the Right to Buy.

CHAPTER NINE

Moving to a fairer system of affordable social rents

Our Key Measures are:

- To keep social rents at an affordable level, well below those in the private sector

- To limit registered social landlords' overall annual rent increases to a maximum of ½ per cent above inflation from 2002/03

- To allow slightly quicker increases in local authority rents, reflecting ongoing improvements in the quality of local authority homes and achieving consistency in the approach to rent setting between the local authority and registered social landlord sectors

- To implement a system of rent setting under which rents reflect property size, value and local earnings

- To achieve a coherent structure for social rents within 10 years, but to give landlords some flexibility over detailed implementation

- To fully compensate the majority of tenants for rent changes through Housing Benefit, and encourage social landlords to ensure that no changes in rents as a result of restructuring are more than £2 per week in any year above the normal inflation-linked increase

---

What the Green Paper said

9.1 Chapter 10 of the Green Paper presented our proposals for the future level of social rents and options for reform of their structure. It argued that there is no case for a substantial change in the average level of social rents, but set out a variety of options for bringing greater fairness and coherence to their structure, so that comparable homes within the same area attract comparable rents.

9.2 In the Green Paper we explained that our objectives for social rents are:

- to ensure that rents remain affordable in the long term;

- to make rents fairer and less confusing for tenants;

- to provide a closer link between rents and the qualities which tenants value in properties;

- to give tenants the opportunity to take more responsibility for their choice of housing while protecting the vulnerable amongst them;

- to reduce unjustifiable differences between the rents set by local authorities and by registered social landlords;

- to encourage better management by social landlords of their stock; and

- to complement our wider objectives to improve quality and choice.

9.3 The Green Paper discussed a number of alternative options for reforming the structure of social rents. It identified three main options which it suggested offered the most promising way forward. These were:

- setting relativities between rents on individual properties using a formula with a weight of 50% on property values and 50% on regional average earnings (the "50/50 option")

- setting rents using a similar formula to the 50/50 option, but changing the weights to 70% on earnings and 30% on property values (the "70/30 option")

- an option under which rents are primarily set on the basis of the running costs of the properties concerned (the "running costs option").

What consultees said

9.4 The responses we received to the Green Paper almost universally agreed on the need to bring more coherence into the structure of social rents. There was less consensus on how this should be achieved, although there was little support for the "running costs" option.

9.5 Five key themes emerged from the consultation responses:

- concern about some of the very high and very low rents which some of the Green Paper's options could produce. For example, some respondents felt that the 50/50 option would create large increases in rents in London which would be unaffordable to tenants;

- worries about the impact on the financial viability of registered social landlords of some of the Green Paper's options;

- the need to give greater attention to affordability considerations in developing the proposals. The National Housing Federation, in particular, argued that the rents charged for different types of properties should take account of the earnings of the types of tenants for whom such homes would be most appropriate;

- the need for social landlords to have considerable discretion over their rents in order to take account of local considerations;

- concerns that the pattern of rents generated by the Green Paper's 70/30 model contained little local variation, and therefore few incentives for tenants to seek accommodation most appropriate to their needs.

Our policy approach

THE AVERAGE LEVEL OF SOCIAL RENTS

9.6 We have considered very carefully the responses to the consultation. We have debated the issues in detail with key players, and commissioned further analysis. In the light of this work, we have amended our proposals on rents from those in the Green Paper in a number of important respects. However, we remain committed to keeping social rents at an affordable level, on average well below those in the private sector.

9.7 Our commitment to keeping social rents at affordable levels has led us to conclude that from 2002/3 the maximum rate of increase in average rents in the registered social landlord sector should be reduced from the current rate of 1% above inflation (RPI+1) to RPI+½ per annum. This rate of increase is slightly faster than proposed in the Green Paper. Registered social landlords and their lenders raised serious concerns about the financial difficulties they would face had future increases in rents been held to RPI+0 and research by KPMG and HACAS Chapman Hendy confirmed that some of their worries were justified. A financially robust registered social landlord sector is critical to the well-being of tenants, and we concluded that it would be right to adjust our original plans.

9.8 In the medium term, we anticipate that average local authority rents will increase at the same rate as those for registered social landlords. In the short term, however, local authority rents will have to increase slightly faster than registered social landlords' rents. This will reflect the major quality improvements being delivered by the extra investment we are making available for homes owned by local authorities, and will reduce the existing gap between local authority and registered social landlord rents. Even so, average local authority and registered social landlord rents will still be increasing less quickly than they have done over the last decade.

9.9 We will review the progress that has been made with the implementation of rent reforms after about three years. The review will have a particular focus on movements in registered social landlords' costs taking into account the efficiency gains which adoption of Best Value should deliver and the implications for our policy on rent increases.

RESTRUCTURING APPROACH

9.10 We have given careful consideration to the comments that were made in response to the alternative restructuring models illustrated in the Green Paper. Devising a coherent structure of social rents has not been easy, given the range of conflicting pressures and objectives. We thought very carefully about the impact of options on landlords and tenants and about issues of affordability.

9.11 We have concluded that linking rents to property values offers a simple and straightforward way of taking account of the size, location and condition of properties but the weight that should be placed on this factor when calculating rents should be 30% and not 50%. The weight placed on local earnings will therefore be 70%. We accept the legitimate concerns that a higher weight on property values would generate excessively high rents which tenants couldn't afford in areas such as London, whilst very low rents in other areas would threaten the viability of many registered social landlords.

9.12   We have also accepted the arguments of a number of respondents that rents should in part reflect property size and have concluded that an additional factor should be included in the model to take greater account of this element. This will help to ensure a sensible pattern of differentials between properties with different numbers of bedrooms, and support our policy of giving more choice to tenants. They will now be able to choose between paying a little less for a smaller home – or a little more to get the benefit of an extra bedroom.

AFFORDABILITY ISSUES

9.13   Some respondents to the Green Paper argued that the structure of rents should be designed to ensure not only that rents, on average, are affordable, but also that particular groups of tenants, such as lone parents or pensioners, face rents which are appropriate to their circumstances. We looked very carefully at the affordability implications of our proposals and compared them with a variety of alternative schemes. We found that no single scheme offered any significant improvement or deterioration in the affordability of rents for any discrete group of tenants. This is because tenants live in a wide variety of different types of home and location. It is therefore not feasible to improve affordability for a particular target group by adjusting the rents charged on particular types of property. Moreover, the varying characteristics of tenants should be reflected in the nature and level of the benefit they receive, rather than their rent, which relates to the property.

FURTHER GUIDANCE

9.14   Precise details of how we propose that social rents should be set in future are set out in 'A Guide to Social Rent Reforms', which is being published today. The Guide should enable landlords and tenants to calculate the implications for them of our policy proposals. In addition, the Housing Corporation will be consulting in early 2001 on the approach it will be taking to implementing the reforms in the registered social landlord sector.

CONVERGENCE

9.15   We want to achieve the right balance between the average rents charged by local authorities and registered social landlords. Our objective is to reach a position where differences in rents between properties in the social housing sector are justified by differences in objective criteria, such as the size and value of properties, and earnings levels, rather than whether the property is owned by a local authority or a registered social landlord.

9.16   This does not mean that it is our objective that average local authority rents will be equal to average registered social landlord rents. Indeed, under the approach to restructuring outlined above it is likely to mean that, reflecting differences particularly in the age of the stock, average local authority rents will remain 5 – 10% below those of registered social landlords. This is rather less than at present. This year's spending review concluded that local authority guideline rents should increase by 2% in real terms in 2001/2, and 1% in real terms in each of the two subsequent years. These increases will make a start on closing the gap with registered social landlord rents. We will review in subsequent spending reviews the rate at which the gap should be closed in later years.

DISCRETION FOR LANDLORDS

9.17   Although we are proposing a single formula to guide landlords in setting rents, we accept that they should have some discretion over the rents that are set for individual properties.

This will allow landlords to take account of local factors and concerns in consultation with tenants. However, it is important that once restructuring is complete the central objective of rent coherence is achieved. We will therefore encourage social landlords to set rents on individual properties which remain normally within a band of up to 5% higher or lower than the target rents suggested by the national approach.

TIMING AND MONITORING

9.18   We propose to stick to the objective set out in the Green Paper that rent restructuring should be completed over a ten year period starting in 2002. Phasing rent restructuring over several years will limit the changes that tenants face in their rent in any one year. We will expect social landlords to ensure that no tenant will be subject to a change in their rent as a result of the combined impact of restructuring and convergence of more than £2 per week in any year above the normal inflation-linked increase. This will significantly lessen the impact on those tenants who will have to meet rent increases out of their own pockets. Together with our reforms of the lettings system, these tenants will also have the option and the opportunity to seek alternative accommodation in the social housing sector, should they wish. We will also allow landlords some discretion over the precise pace and timing of their own rent restructuring, although we do not expect the changes to be concentrated in the later years of the ten year period which we are allowing for restructuring.

9.19   Each social landlord will be expected to produce an annual restructuring progress report covering issues such as the calculation of target rents, plans for attaining the targets over the ten-year implementation period, and progress achieved. Local authority landlords will produce their reports as part of their annual business planning round. The Housing Corporation will be issuing guidance separately about how it intends to monitor implementation within the registered social landlord sector. Landlords may choose to include these reports as part of their business plans or, in the case of registered social landlords, their regulatory returns.

THE IMPACT ON TENANTS

9.20   The restructuring proposals above will result in rent increases or rent reductions for large numbers of properties. Average rent levels in the registered social landlord sector will be increasing by ½% faster than inflation, and local authority rents a little faster than this. However, for individual properties, changes in rents will depend greatly on whether the present rent is above or below the long term target implied by our restructuring formula. Furthermore, the vast majority of tenants will not experience any change in the amount of rent they pay themselves since they will be fully compensated by changes in the amount of Housing Benefit they receive. A full analysis of the impact of our proposals is being published in 'A Guide to Social Rent Reforms'.

PROTECTING REGISTERED SOCIAL LANDLORDS' FINANCES

9.21   It is critically important to tenants of registered social landlords that their homes are properly looked after, and that their landlord remains financially healthy. We recognise that even with national average rents increasing at RPI+½, some registered social landlords, particularly in areas with relatively low property values, may be unable to achieve full rent restructuring within ten years while also fulfilling their obligations to their tenants and funders. Simultaneously with this document, a summary of detailed research by KPMG and HACAS Chapman Hendy into the finances of 40 registered social landlords is being published. It concludes that only a very small proportion of registered social landlords will be prevented for financial reasons from completing their restructuring within ten years. Those which are unable to do so will be subject to a review by the Housing Corporation. If the Corporation accepts that there are legitimate grounds for not achieving the new structure, it will sign off restructuring plans which deliver as much progress as is considered possible. The Housing Corporation will issue guidance early in the New Year to registered social landlords setting out, in detail, how it intends to approach the regulation of rent restructuring.

LARGE SCALE VOLUNTARY TRANSFERS

9.22   Past agreements governing the large-scale voluntary transfer of local authority housing to registered social landlords, including those for properties due to be transferred as part of this year's programme, have often provided guarantees to tenants that their rents will not increase by more than a set amount for a certain period, typically RPI+1 for five years. These are important guarantees which must be honoured. Commitments to lenders which may also depend on the registered social landlords charging a particular pattern or level of rents must also be honoured. If, after these commitments have been met, there remains scope to make progress on rent restructuring, we will expect landlords to do so. Transfers that take place in the 2001 programme and beyond will be expected to achieve convergence and restructuring to the same timetable as other social housing stock.

NEIGHBOURHOOD RENEWAL

9.23   We value the contribution that registered social landlords are making to regeneration and wish to see this continue. We believe that registered social landlords should, and can, play an important part in neighbourhood renewal and in preventing decline:

- they share a key responsibility with local authorities for delivering housing targets for deprived areas, and in using lettings policies to create more sustainable communities;

- they have an important role to play in working with local authorities and others in Local Strategic Partnerships, which in the 88 most deprived local authority districts will be funded through the Neighbourhood Renewal Fund. With the agreement of the partnership, they could act as the lead implementation body;

- in some areas they may be well placed to take a lead in Neighbourhood Management or Neighbourhood Warden schemes, both of which have dedicated streams of funding.

9.24   Notwithstanding the important role we see for registered social landlords in regeneration and renewal, we do not accept that our rent restructuring proposals should be adjusted in order to provide extra rental income for those operating in regeneration areas. To do so would imply that poorer members of society who live in the most deprived areas should pay higher rents in order to fund their own regeneration. We expect non-housing activity to be funded by the relevant main programme, and will actively support and encourage registered social landlords to seek such funding. At the same time, where registered social landlords can contribute to preventative or regeneration activities, which maintain the quality of the neighbourhood for tenants and enhance the value of the stock, it remains open to them to use some of their rental income to contribute to these.

SERVICE CHARGES

9.25   The material on rents in the Housing Green Paper deliberately focused on the property element of rents. However, we are keen that service charges including support charges for the Supporting People programme are also levied on consistent and transparent principles.

9.26   Service charges reflect services provided to tenants which are not governed by the same factors as the property element of rents. The restructuring formula discussed above will not apply to the charges levied for these services. We propose a different approach for this element.

9.27   We expect landlords to ensure that service charges closely reflect what is being provided to tenants. The Housing Corporation will issue guidance in early 2001 which will encourage registered social landlords to examine carefully the balance between rents and service charges within the context of the existing legislative and regulatory framework, and to make any necessary changes. This guidance will also cover support charges eligible for Transitional Housing Benefit, which will parallel similar guidance being issued to large-scale voluntary transfer authorities and to local housing authorities by DETR. From 2002/03, the Corporation's rent-influencing policy will aim to ensure that increases in the overall quantum of rents and service charges for registered social landlords is limited to RPI+½. In looking at individual registered social landlords, the Corporation will need to be able to distinguish between rents, which would be expected to change by RPI+½, plus or minus any adjustments for rent restructuring, and service charges, which would normally be expected to change simply by RPI+½. Some additional flexibility may be needed in relation to support charges and supported housing, in line with the Housing Corporation's current guidance. Local authority landlords will also be expected to set service charges which are reasonable and transparent. As part of the Supporting People programme we will be issuing guidance to both registered social landlords and local authorities on support charges prior to 2003.

SUPPLEMENTARY GUIDE

9.28   'A Guide to Social Rent Reforms' is being issued today. It provides:

- guidance to help individual social landlords and tenants to determine how the restructuring approach affects their own rents;

- an analysis of the implications for landlords and tenants of our changes; and

- a discussion of some of the more detailed issues surrounding the implementation of rent restructuring.

CHAPTER TEN

Improving Housing Benefit

Our Key Measures are:

- To raise standards in Housing Benefit administration and promote work incentives, working with local authorities;

- To set up an expert-team to help struggling local authorities tackle immediate problems, along with action to improve the situation of registered social landlords;

- To develop and implement a new performance management framework to raise standards across the board and link local authority performance to funding;

- To promote work incentives for young people through reform of the Single Room Rent;

- To make Housing Benefit both easier to administer and easier to claim by streamlining and simplifying the process for making claims, and ensuring the rules are compatible with Tax Credits;

- To simplify Housing Benefit by further exploring simplification of the 4 transitional protection schemes.

What the Green Paper said

10.1   Chapter 11 of the Green Paper set out the problems that we inherited with Housing Benefit. It set out initiatives that are already underway to make the scheme work better, and put forward further ideas for improving customer service, reducing fraud and error, and helping reduce the barriers to work. It also invited views on possible options for more fundamental structural change in the longer-term.

What consultees said

10.2   There was widespread acceptance among respondents of the analysis presented in the Green Paper, and the need for reform. A significant number of respondents felt that the current administration of Housing Benefit was facing severe problems and that this should be the priority for action.

10.3   Respondents generally welcomed our objectives and supported the measures in hand to deliver improvements. Proposals to use better information sharing and a single claims process to improve customer service were widely welcomed. There was also support for possible options for simplifying the current scheme.

10.4   Support for proposals for tackling fraud and error was accompanied by concerns that delays in processing claims were arising in some local authorities as they implemented new anti-fraud initiatives. There was widespread support for taking action to improve work incentives, and in particular for reform of the Single Room Rent. Finally, there was general support for longer-term, more structural reform but varying views about when it should take place, and in what form.

Our policy approach

10.5 Housing Benefit has an important role both in terms of our welfare to work and social exclusion agenda and wider housing objectives in Great Britain. We have listened and have concluded that there is the need for action on two main fronts:

- to **raise standards in administration** – by raising standards across the board, but also helping struggling authorities improve; and

- to **simplify the system** – by reforming the Single Room Rent and exploring scope for simplifying both the claims process and the 4 parallel schemes that are currently in place.

10.6 Action on both these fronts will promote both better administration and better work incentives.

10.7 In addition, we are giving further consideration to options for reforming housing support over the long-term. For example, by looking in more detail at the issues raised by respondents commenting on a scheme with a flat-rate element, as well as listening to ideas that will be raised as part of our consultation on the Pension Credit.

THE PROBLEMS WE INHERITED

10.8 There is no question that the fundamental challenge facing Housing Benefit today is its administration. That is why this issue is our immediate priority.

10.9 There are 409 local authorities administering Housing Benefit. Some do a difficult job well. But a number struggle.

10.10 Problems with administering Housing Benefit can result in unacceptable levels of fraud and error, as well as backlogs of delayed claims. Because people lack confidence in the system they worry that Housing Benefit won't get sorted quickly if they lose their job or have to make a new claim on entering work. Indeed, at the present time, much of the work disincentive effect lies in the administrative problems, rather than the design of the scheme itself.

10.11 In addition, delays to paying benefits affect vulnerable groups, like pensioners. Tenants worry about paying their rent if their benefit takes a long time to come through. Landlords also experience cash flow problems, which often deter private landlords from renting to people getting Housing Benefit. Problems administering the system also undermine our efforts to drive down fraud and error.

10.12 Simply taking the administration of Housing Benefit away from local authorities would not resolve the current problems. Some local authorities do a good job in administering Housing Benefit. The best way to resolve the present situation is to improve the standard of those local authorities which have fallen behind.

10.13   The reasons for problems in Housing Benefit administration are many and varied. Too often Housing Benefit has not been a priority for local authorities. Too many councillors are unaware of the problems their local service faces. This has often resulted in neglected services, suffering from under-investment. It is no coincidence that local authorities which see Housing Benefit as one of their strategic priorities tend to deliver better services.

10.14   In addition, Housing Benefit itself is part of the problem. It is complex to administer. Successive governments have layered complexity onto complexity, usually to avoid people 'losing out' as the result of new changes. As a result, we now have four Housing Benefit schemes running in parallel. Central government has also been slow to set clear standards for Housing Benefit delivery and has not worked in partnership with local authorities to ensure the public get a quality service. We have started to change that.

RAISING STANDARDS – DELIVERING QUALITY SERVICES IN HOUSING BENEFIT

10.15   The Best Value regime has set out the five key areas for performance, including targets for the time within which local authorities must process people's claims, the accuracy of their decisions and the action they need to take to tackle fraud. This gives us the basis for moving towards consistent national standards.

10.16   We have also just announced the first increase in funding since 1993. Coupled with that, we are setting local authorities' funding for the next 3 years, allowing authorities to plan ahead in a way that has never been possible before.

10.17   On top of that, we have listened to local authority representations on the extent of the changes we are asking them to deliver and the need for a stable base from which to raise performance. We want to strike a proper balance between the need to clear backlogs of claims and provide benefit quickly, with the need to introduce improvements in areas such as fraud.

10.18   We are determined to protect benefits against fraud. We are working with 10 local authorities to pilot a fraud hotline from January 2001. Our new anti-fraud incentive scheme is being introduced to further secure the gateway to Housing Benefit and put the focus on prevention, as well as detection. The old scheme only rewarded detection and used a weak measure. Good authorities that checked claims properly and so had less fraud could be penalised. The new scheme sets out the anti-fraud activities we expect local authorities to undertake. And it introduces more generous financial rewards to local authorities who act to prevent fraud happening in the first place. We have listened to local authority representations about their capacity to implement the scheme next year and have agreed to run the new scheme alongside the old for 1 year, allowing local authorities some choice and flexibility around its implementation.

10.19   We have also listened to the issues that local authorities face in implementing the new Verification Framework (designed to strengthen identity checks). So, we have already introduced greater flexibility to it. In addition, from 2002, we are breaking the framework down into separate parts that will allow local authorities to introduce it incrementally.

10.20   We are also working to support local authorities in delivering a better service to tenants and landlords by providing new IT tools to improve the sharing of information between DSS and local authorities. This will provide data in a more user-friendly format, and will widen the range of benefits information that local authorities can access to include, for example, Incapacity Benefit and Retirement Pension. We are doing that by working to modernise existing arrangements and provide a new 'Integrated Enquiry Service'. By providing access to our central system for National Insurance numbers (DCI) we are also bolstering local authorities' efforts to tackle fraud.

10.21   We are also determined to provide local authorities with clearer, better, and more co-ordinated guidance and circulars. Because we are prioritising action to improve performance and tackle fraud we have decided, after consultation with local authorities, to temporarily hold off from introducing the new appeals rules and to leave the Housing Benefit and Council Tax Benefit backdating rules as they are.

10.22   These measures are providing the foundation for a better service. Striking a balance – focusing in on priority changes that will make the most difference, at the same limiting the number of changes so that we support local authorities in their efforts to improve the services they deliver.

10.23   In addition, local authorities and their partners are working hard to look at not just what central government can do to make Housing Benefit easier for them to administer, but what they can do to help themselves deliver it better.

10.24   The next sections of this chapter set out our proposals for further action to raise performance. First, we want immediate action to tackle problems in the most acutely affected areas. Second, we want to work with local authorities to develop a 'performance framework' that will put Housing Benefit on a firmer footing and raise standards across the board.

HELPING STRUGGLING LOCAL AUTHORITIES GET BACK ON TRACK

10.25   As well as looking to simplify the system and raise standards across the board, we will act to help tackle the acute problems that some local authorities are currently struggling with. There is already a good deal of work being done by I&DeA (the local government Improvement and Development Agency), BFI (Benefit Fraud Inspectorate) and others on sharing good practice. We want to build on this by targeting specific help on local authorities who need immediate help.

10.26   Local authorities are responsible for the quality of services they deliver. But we are determined to play our part in making sure the public get the service they deserve. So, struggling local authorities will get access to an expert help-team.

10.27   This team will, in the first instance, work with a small number of local authorities to identify what is going wrong and what action they need to take to sort things out. The team will help local authorities access resources for clearing up immediate problems, such as backlogs. But they will also help local authorities prevent problems recurring through the development and implementation of local improvement plans.

10.28   We are committing £2 million to fund the team and its work. In turn, we are looking for local authorities to work with us and play an active role. In particular, we want to build on the contribution of the Beacons Service by looking to involve successful local authorities in helping their struggling counterparts.

10.29   We are now discussing how to take this forward with local authorities, their representatives and IdeA.

10.30   We are also mindful of the need to alleviate the problems that claim backlogs cause for social landlords. Registered social landlords, who often provide housing for the most deprived in society, account for about 20% of Housing Benefit cases, and some of them are experiencing acute cash flow problems due to delays. Some registered social landlords have volunteered to undertake elements of Housing Benefit administration in order to help their tenants, ease their cash flow and relieve some pressure from local authorities. We are discussing with them what their detailed proposals are and what they might mean in practice.

PERFORMANCE FRAMEWORK

10.31   While we are determined to act now to help tackle the worst problems, we also want to look at improving performance across the board. That is why we will develop a 'performance framework' to support the improved delivery of Housing Benefit and better manage the planning and implementation of changes to the system.

10.32   This framework would build on Best Value. But we want to develop the current measures so that they provide a set of consistent national standards that are backed up by accurate and timely management information. Local authorities will know what they are expected to deliver. We will know how they are doing. And because we want the public to know we will look to publish league tables. We also want to explore how we could develop an administration subsidy regime that, for the first time, links payments for administration to performance.

10.33   Together these measures provide a stable basis on which local authorities can plan, invest and deliver the standard of service the public deserve.

SIMPLIFYING THE SCHEME – PROMOTING WORK INCENTIVES AND BETTER ADMINISTRATION

10.34   Housing Benefit is complicated. This makes it difficult for local authorities to administer and difficult for the public to understand. That, in turn, makes it more vulnerable to fraud and error and damages work incentives.

10.35   The Green Paper set out a wide range of ideas for possible reform. The responses were broadly positive. We now want to focus our efforts on some key areas, including:

- reform of the Single Room Rent rules;

- introduction of a more effective process for making claims, along with changes to ease the transition into work and improve the administrative fit between Housing Benefit and tax credits; and

- possible simplification of transitional schemes.

REFORMING THE SINGLE ROOM RENT

10.36   There was considerable support for many of the possible measures we discussed to improve work incentives. In particular, many consultees argued for the outright abolition of the Single Room Rent (although this was not proposed).

10.37   We have given these views careful consideration. It would be wrong for the benefit system to provide unemployed young adults with better housing than their working peers could afford. But we agree that young people need to be able to access reasonable accommodation so that they can concentrate their efforts on finding work.

10.38   We are therefore proceeding with our proposals to broaden the definition of the Single Room Rent. This will both ease the problems faced by young people in getting and maintaining accommodation, and encourage landlords to rent to young adults.

10.39   We know that many respondents want this reform introduced as quickly as possible. We will press ahead with developing the detail and the regulations, in consultation with the relevant parties. Given the need to complete this work, the earliest this reform could be introduced is April 2001. We will discuss the exact timing with local authorities before taking a final decision.

IMPROVING THE CLAIMS PROCESS

10.40   We recognise that some of the current arrangements for claiming benefits get in the way of good administration and undermine work incentives.

10.41   People claiming Housing Benefit, together with social security benefits or tax credits, have to complete multiple, lengthy paper claim forms. They also have to provide (with evidence) the same information to the different organisations involved. This can create delay and frustration for the claimant and duplication for the organisations involved.

10.42   That is why, as part of the new Working Age Agency, we are developing a new process for people claiming Income Support, Job Seeker's Allowance and Incapacity Benefit. Any information specific to Housing Benefit (such as their rent and tenancy agreement) could be collected at the same time as the person claims IS, JSA or IB. So the claimant will have to give the information once, and only once.

10.43   In addition, to remove the need to complete lengthy paper forms, information will mainly be gathered over the telephone or face-to-face. Where possible, we will also check the evidence required for Housing Benefit. Local authority staff would then complete the process by referring cases to the Rent Officer (if necessary), calculating entitlement and paying the Housing Benefit. We will work with local authorities to trial this process so that we extend the co-operation that already exists between local authorities, the Benefits Agency and Employment Service Offices in some areas, and make sure the right IT tools to do the job are in place.

10.44   We are also developing a dedicated service for **pensioners** along the same lines as set out above. And our new pensions organisation will have a key part to play.

SIMPLIFYING CHANGE OF CIRCUMSTANCES AND FIXED PERIOD AWARDS

10.45   We are also convinced of the need to simplify both the process of awarding Housing Benefit, and how we deal with changes to peoples' circumstances.

10.46   Housing Benefit is awarded for specific periods, usually 6 or 12 months, after which people have to start again, filling in a completely new form and going through the whole claim process in its entirety. This can act as a disincentive for some groups, like pensioners, to claim at all. People who are in work and getting help through tax credits get confused by the different rules. It is also an additional burden on local authorities.

10.47   There are at least 3 specific changes that we want to introduce:

- **Ease the transition into work, for example by removing the need to make a new claim for Housing Benefit on starting work.** Instead, this could be treated as a change of circumstances so speedier payment can be achieved.

- **Speed up getting Housing Benefit paid if a job ends after a short period** by confirming their details using a simplified, shorter claim form.

- **Ease the payment of Housing Benefit to pensioners** by removing the requirement for them to make new claims every year, instead allowing simpler reviews so that benefit can be adjusted if their circumstances change.

10.48   We will work with local authorities to develop the detail and discuss the timing for the introduction of these improvements.

10.49   On a related point, throughout the period when Housing Benefit is being paid, people are obliged to report <u>all</u> changes in their circumstances, however small. Over 60% of claimants will have at least one change of circumstance that affects their benefit entitlement over the course of a year (excluding the uprating of benefit). Dealing with all these changes can be costly, lead to delays and overpayments, and result in a good deal of frustration. Yet over half of these changes affect the amount of benefit paid by less than £2 a week.

10.50   So we want to look at what we can do in this area. We want to explore the scope for greater flexibility in the handling of changes of circumstances and in the setting of awards. Our consultation paper on the Pension Credit proposed looking at longer, fixed awards and abolishing weekly means tests. We want to see how Housing Benefit might fit into this framework.

SIMPLIFICATION

10.51   The Green Paper described the administrative difficulties that arise because local authorities operate four different schemes to restrict rent eligible for Housing Benefit in the private rented sector. Two of the schemes were designed to 'transitionally protect' tenants from rule changes introduced in the past. Which scheme applies to which claimant depends on the date from which they first claimed Housing Benefit. In addition, this complexity is compounded by additional rules layered on over time.

10.52   Our reform of the Single Room Rent has been covered separately. We want to look further at scope for additional simplification in this area. We intend to do some further analysis to see what the full range of options are. Again, we will work with local authorities in taking this forward.

TAKING REFORMS FORWARD

10.53   There is a need to strike the right balance between building on reforms already made and introducing more change. We are not ruling out making other improvements, but the proposals set out here deliberately focus on areas we think could contribute most, at this time, to easing the administrative burden, promoting work, and improving services to customers. There is never any shortage of ideas for improving Housing Benefit. But there is a shortage of capacity in local authorities to implement them. Every improvement is an additional change for local authorities to manage. That is why we want to focus on quality not quantity and work with local authorities to improve the system and its delivery.

10.54 There were a number of changes raised in the Green Paper which we don't intend to pursue at this time. These include further reform of disregards, tapers and non-dependent deductions. Given the current problems, sorting out the administration, combined with our 'benefit run-ons', will have more impact on work incentives than changing additional rules in these areas.

10.55 For those key measures that we are pursuing, we will now work with local authorities, housing providers and others to:

- develop the detail of the proposals; and

- identify which of the measures to introduce first, and when.

Looking to the Long-term

10.56 The Green Paper also discussed some fundamental reforms to Housing Benefit that might be introduced in the longer-term. The aim of such reforms would be to give tenants more of an interest in their rent, and help promote quality and choice in the rented-sector. The options considered were housing tax credits, a scheme with a flat rate element, and bonus payments for claimants living in cheaper than average properties.

10.57 Among respondents there was much support for longer-term reform, but most agreed with the Green Paper that the introduction of any shopping incentives should wait until rents in the social housing sector were reformed. Also, respondents expressed a number of concerns about a flat rate housing element or bonus payment.

10.58 On the issue of introducing a scheme with a flat-rate element, we are considering the views of respondents. We want to consider this option further. But we also want to develop proposals for possible reform of housing support for people of working age and pensioners in line with our different objectives for these groups.

10.59 For **pensioners**, we have recently issued the consultation paper on the Pension Credit and we are already committed to improving the service to pensioners, but await views on how housing support should be delivered within that framework. We would be interested in whether people favour paying Housing Benefit separately to the Credit (as currently envisaged), or as part of it.

10.60 So, we are considering options for long-term reform. But, because of the priorities we have set out here, we believe it is right – in the short and medium term – to focus on improving the administration and simplifying where possible before implementing long-term structural changes to the system.

CHAPTER ELEVEN

Tackling other forms of social exclusion

Our Key Measures are:

- To cut the number of rough sleepers by two thirds by 2002
- To introduce Supporting People in 2003, preceded by a new Safer Communities Supported Housing Fund
- To consult on a fuel poverty strategy by the end of the year
- To refurbish and improve existing local authority Gypsy sites
- To take forward the recommendations of Policy Action Team 8 to tackle anti-social behaviour

What the Green Paper said

11.1   In the Housing Green Paper we emphasised the important role of housing policies in our strategy to tackle all forms of social exclusion. We set out in Chapter 12 of the Green Paper the policies we were putting in place to tackle other forms of housing-related social exclusion.

What consultees said

11.2   Those who responded to Chapter 12 of the Green Paper generally welcomed its principles, in particular the recognition that housing had a key role to play in individual well-being and community stability.

Our policy approach

ROUGH SLEEPING

11.3   The Rough Sleepers Unit was set up in 1998 to deliver the Prime Minister's challenging target of reducing the number of people sleeping rough in England to as near to zero as possible and by at least two thirds by 2002. The Unit has now put in place all the services outlined in its strategy Coming in from the Cold. Indications are that the Unit is on track to deliver the target. Street count results this Summer showed that the numbers of people sleeping on the street had fallen by a third since 1998.

11.4   We will continue to focus our effort on the most vulnerable groups and to target the underlying causes of the problem. Outside London we are working closely with local authorities and especially those in the 33 areas with the largest number of rough sleepers.

We recently announced an additional £9.5 million for services in these areas. Across the country, to date, we have:

- established Contact and Assessment teams in central London and other major cities;

- provided an additional 800 hostel spaces for vulnerable rough sleepers in London;

- provided an extra £1 million to combat drug misuse by rough sleepers in London and £800,000 in areas outside London which have significant numbers of drug addicted rough sleepers;

- established Tenancy Sustainment Teams in central London and other major cities to help former rough sleepers move into independent living, with work, education, or training opportunities;

- announced £2.4 million for projects across the country designed to give a better future for former rough sleepers.

11.5   We remain committed to preventing a new generation of rough sleepers. The Rough Sleepers Unit is working with other Government Departments to improve statutory and administrative arrangements to help particularly vulnerable groups. The Unit is also funding a wide range of measures across the country to prevent rough sleeping at the local level. These include specific work in rural areas, with vulnerable groups such as careleavers, and with people leaving the armed forces. Our proposals on homelessness (described earlier in this statement) complement our programme to reduce and prevent rough sleeping.

SUPPORTING PEOPLE

11.6   The new Supporting People programme will be implemented in 2003. The aim of this programme is to improve the quality, range and flexibility of support services to vulnerable people. It will achieve this through focusing provision on local need, integrating 'support' with wider local strategies and monitoring quality and effectiveness both in urban and rural areas.

11.7   We are working closely with service providers, local authorities and other stakeholders to develop the framework of the programme and the implementation plan. This involves wide consultation both with a variety of key stakeholders, and a series of consultation papers. To date papers have been published on managing the changeover, phasing, decision making and working arrangements, and monitoring and quality, with further papers planned on charging and the allocations formula. In addition, a consolidation paper on the outcome of consultation so far will be published in January.

11.8   We are committed to the success of this policy and will provide £138 million in funds for the implementation of the policy over the next three years. For next year, over £15 million will be made directly available to local authorities for setting up Supporting People implementation teams in each area. These teams will begin the work of assessing current supply and setting up shadow strategic bodies. In addition, money is being made available to provider organisations to help providers and agencies in understanding and discharging their new roles.

11.9   Finally, through the Safer Communities Supported Housing Fund, new money will be made available to ensure that services can expand in the run up to implementation. This fund of £137 million over the next three years will generate additional services for people fleeing domestic violence, ex-offenders, drug and alcohol users and young people at risk.

FUEL POVERTY

11.10   The new Home Energy Efficiency Scheme was launched in June following publication of the Housing Green Paper in April. The programme has already begun to improve homes in England by offering insulation and central heating packages worth up to £2,000 to fuel-poor households.

11.11   In November 1999 an Inter-ministerial Group on Fuel Poverty was set up to take a strategic overview of the policies and initiatives with a bearing on fuel poverty and to develop and publish a UK Strategy setting out fuel poverty objectives and targets and the policies to deliver them. The consultation draft of the Strategy is due to be published by the end of the year.

11.12   We published the UK's climate change programme on 17 November 2000. The programme details a number of measures that will help to reduce fuel poverty, as well as levels of greenhouse gas emissions, including the new Home Energy Efficiency Scheme, a new Energy Efficiency Commitment scheme for 2002-2005, the Affordable Warmth Programme and support for the replacement of community heating systems.

11.13   Our programmes for private housing renovation and quality improvements in social housing will also play a key role in improving the energy efficiency of our housing stock and tackling fuel poverty.

GYPSIES

11.14   Whilst the focus in the Green Paper itself was on traditional forms of housing, we recognise the particular needs of those Gypsies who follow a nomadic way of life. As a result of the Spending Review, we announced that £17 million would be made available to local authorities over the next three years for the refurbishment and improvement of the existing network of some 300 local authority Gypsy sites. This will improve the quality of life for the residents of those sites and extend the useful life of the sites themselves. The scheme will take the form of an annual bidding round and guidance and invitations to apply for 2001/02 were recently sent out to all local authorities. In addition we are about to commission research into the availability and condition of sites, including how they are managed, as a means of assessing the need for further sites, and to inform the next spending review.

TACKLING CRIME AND ANTI-SOCIAL BEHAVIOUR

11.15   We recognise the very important role that good housing provision and management has in tackling crime and anti-social behaviour. The Home Office is co-ordinating the national drive against anti-social behaviour, working with DETR and other Government Departments. It has set up a working group to take forward the Social Exclusion Unit's Policy Action Team 8 action plan on tackling anti-social behaviour. Crime and Disorder Partnerships in each local authority area will be taking the lead role in tackling anti-social behaviour on the ground. Each Partnership has drawn up a strategy, based on the views of local residents, to tackle crime and disorder and they are to receive special funding, in the form of £160 million per year over 2001 to 2004 to implement the strategies, focussing on high-crime areas.

11.16   A number of our proposals for the private rented sector (described earlier in this statement) will help to tackle anti-social behaviour. These include our proposals for best practice guidance on landlord accreditation schemes, provision of low cost management services and licensing of landlords in areas of low demand and benefit measures linked to our licensing proposals. We will take these forward in 2001.

11.17   Policy Action Team 6 also identified the introduction of neighbourhood wardens as a visible, recognisable presence to deter crime and low-level anti-social behaviour. A Neighbourhood Wardens Unit has been set up in the DETR and £13.5 million has been allocated over the next three years to fund new schemes and support existing ones.

Conclusion

11.18   We want everyone to have the opportunity of a decent home. We want people to have real choices over where they live. Where people aspire to home ownership our policies can help them do so and will improve the buying and selling process. For the private rented sector our policies will support responsible landlords and tenants and enable effective action against unscrupulous landlords. In social housing, our policies will ensure that all homes are decent and that tenants have more choice and more of a say in the management of their homes. Our policies will give local authorities more freedoms and flexibilities to develop local strategies and manage their stock in a way that is right for their tenants and residents. And we have backed up our policies with resources – more than doubling the level of housing investment by 2004 compared to spending plans for 1997/98. This policy statement sets out our strategy to deliver improvements in quality and choice in housing and will play a major part in our strategy for tackling all forms of social exclusion.

11.19   We now look to those in the private, public and voluntary sectors to join us over the next decade and beyond in implementing these policies and ensuring that everyone has the opportunity, and choice, of a decent home.

INDEX OF RELATED DOCUMENTS

Quality and Choice: A decent home for all – Summary – The way forward for housing

Available on DETR website at: www.detr.gov.uk/housing

Product code: 0 HC00 1156
Paper copies – gratis from DETR Free Literature, PO Box 236, Wetherby LS23 7NB,
Tel 0870 1226 236, Fax: 0870 1226 237, Email: detr@twoten.press.net

Quality and Choice : A decent home for all – The housing green paper

Available on DETR website at: www.detr.gov.uk/housing

Paper copies available from DETR publications sales centre at the address at the front
of this document, DETR, ISBN 1 85112 378 4, £10

Quality and Choice : A decent home for all – The housing green paper – Summary

Product code 0 HC 0021
Paper copies – gratis from DETR Free Literature, PO Box 236, Wetherby LS23 7NB,
Tel 0870 1226 236, Fax: 0870 1226 237, Email: detr@twoten.press.net

The Housing Green Paper, Analysis of Responses

Available on DETR website at: www.detr.gov.uk/housing

The Housing Green Paper, analysis of responses- Summary

Product code 0 HC 00 157
Paper copies – gratis from DETR Free Literature, PO Box 236, Wetherby LS23 7NB,
Tel 0870 1226 236, Fax: 0870 1226 237, Email: detr@twoten.press.net

Urban White Paper, 'Our Towns and Cities – the Future'

Available on DETR website at:
www.regeneration.detr.gov.uk/policies/ourtowns/index.htm

Paper copies available from the Stationery Office, PO Box 29, Norwich NR3 1GN

The State of English Cities, DETR, 2000-12-08

Available on DETR website at:
www.regeneration.detr.gov.uk/policies/ourtowns/index.htm

Paper copies available from DETR publications sales centre at the address at the front
of this document.

Living in Urban England: Attitudes and Aspriations, DETR, 2000

Available on DETR website at:
www.regeneration.detr.gov.uk/policies/ourtowns/index.htm

Paper copies available from DETR publications sales centre at the address at the front
of this document.

Rural White Paper, 'Our Countryside – the Future'

> Available on DETR website at:
> www.wildlife-countryside.detr.gov.uk/ruralwp/index.htm

> Paper copies available from the Stationery Office, PO Box 29, Norwich NR3 1GN

National Strategy for Neighbourhood Renewal

> Available on the Cabinet Office website:
> www.cabinet-office.gov.uk/seu/index/publishe.htm

Draft Bill on Leasehold/Commonhold reform

> Available on Houses of Parliament website at:
> www.publications.parliament.uk/pa/cm/cmpubns.htm

Rethinking Construction – The Report of the Construction Task Force

> Available on DETR website at: www.detr.gov.uk/construction

The Homes Bill

> www.publications.parliament.uk/pa/cm/cmpubns.htm

Explanatory Material Available on DETR website at: www.detr.gov.uk/housing

Chapter 1 – Making it Work Locally

Local Housing Needs Assessment – A Guide to Good Practice

> Available from the DETR Publication Sales Centre from the address at the front of
> this publication.
> Summary available on the DETR website at: www.detr.gov.uk/housing

Collecting, Managing and Using Housing Stock Information – A Good Practice Guide

> Available from the DETR Publication Sales Centre from the address at the front of
> this publication.
> Summary available on the DETR website at: www.detr.gov.uk/housing

Developing Housing Strategies in Rural Areas: A Good Practice Guide
(T Brown, HAR Hunt & B Line).

> Published by the CIoH, The Countryside Agency and the Housing Corporation:
> ISBN 1 900 396 84 X

Chapter 2 – Encouraging Sustainable Home Ownership

Starter Home Initiative Factsheet and Bidding Guidance

> Available on DETR website at: www.detr.gov.uk/housing
> Paper copies available from the DETR on 020-7944 3164

Chapter 3 – Promoting a Healthy Private Rented Sector

Housing Health and Safety Rating System: The Guidance (Version 1)

Available from the DETR publication sales centre from the address at the front of this document.

Housing Research Summary 122 available on the DETR website at: www.detr.gov.uk/housing. Paper copies available from the Housing Support Unit : Tel 020 7944 3257

Housing Health and Safety Rating System : Report on Development

Available from the DETR publication sales centre from the address at the front of this document.

Housing Research Summary 123, available on the DETR website at: www.detr.gov.uk/housing. Paper copies available from the Housing Support Unit: Tel 020 7944 3257

Chapter 4 – Raising the Quality of Social Housing

New Financial Framework Guidance

Available on DETR website at: www.detr.gov.uk/housing
Paper copies available from the DETR on 020-7944 3572

Arms-Length Management of Local Authority Housing: A Consultation Paper

Available on DETR website at: www.detr.gov.uk/housing
Paper copies available from DETR Free Literature Centre, PO Box 236, Wetherby LS23 7NB, Tel: 0870 1226 236

Housing Transfer Guidance for Applicants for 2001 Programme

Available on DETR website at: www.detr.gov.uk/housing
Paper copies available from the DETR on 020-7944 3618

Supplementary Guidance for Applicants

Available on DETR website at: www.detr.gov.uk/housing
Paper copies available from the DETR on 020-7944 3618

Housing Investment Programme Guidance Note

Available on DETR website at: www.detr.gov.uk/housing
Paper copies available from the DETR on 020-7944 3576

Communities in Control

Available on Housing Corporation Website at: www.housingcorp.gov.uk/pubs/documents.htm

Chapter 5 – Providing New Affordable Housing

Planning Policy Guidance Note 3: Housing

> Available on DETR website at: www.detr.gov.uk/planning
> Or from the Stationery Office PO Box 29, Norwich NR3 1GN

Planning Policy Circular 6/98

> Available on DETR website at: www.detr.gov.uk/planning
> Or from the Stationery Office PO Box 29, Norwich NR3 1GN

Chapter 6 – Promoting Choice Through Lettings in Social Housing

Local Authority Policy and Practice on Allocutions, Transfers and Homelessness (Housing Research Summary No. 139)

> Available on DETR website at: www.detr.gov.uk/housing
> Paper copies available from the Housing Support Unit 020 7944 3257

Chapter 9 – Moving to a Fairer System of Affordable Social Rents

A Guide to Social Rent Reforms

> Available on the DETR website at: www.detr.gov.uk/housing
> Or from the DETR on 020-7944 3273

Assessing the Impact of Housing Green Paper Rent Reform Policies on Individual Registered Social Landlords (A paper by KPMG and HACAS Chapman Hendy)

> Available on DETR website at: www.detr.gov.uk/housing
> Paper copies available from the Housing Support Unit 020 7944 3257

Housing Quality Indicators Forms (Version 2) and Scoring Spreadsheet

> Available on the DETR website at www.detr.gov.uk/housing
> Paper copies and spreadsheet diskettes available from DETR publication sales centre at the address at the front of this document, priced £10.

Chapter 11 – Tackling Other Forms of Social Exclusion

Coming in from the Cold and Progress Reports on its Implementation

> Available on the DETR website at www.detr.gov.uk/housing
> Or from the DETR publication sales centre at the address given at the front of this document